Money in Modern Social Encyclicals

Polish Studies in Economics

Edited by Ryszard Kokoszczyński

Volume 16

Piotr Karaś

Money in Modern Social Encyclicals

PETER LANG

Berlin - Bruxelles - Chennai - Lausanne - New York - Oxford

Bibliographic Information published by the Deutsche Nationalbibliothek
The Deutsche Nationalbibliothek lists this publication in the Deutsche Nationalbibliografie; detailed bibliographic data is available in the internet at http://dnb.d-nb.de.

Library of Congress Cataloging-in-Publication Data
A CIP catalog record for this book has been applied for at the Library of Congress.

This publication was financially supported by Krakow University of Economics.

The English edition of this book is based on the following German edition,
Piotr Karaś. Geld in modernen Sozialenzykliken.
Wien: LIT Verlag, 2022, Vol. 40. Wirtschaftswissenschaften.

ISSN 2191-8848
ISBN 978-3-631-91839-5 (Print)
E-ISBN 978-3-631-92193-7 (E-PDF)
E-ISBN 978-3-631-92194-4 (E-PUB)
DOI 10.3726/b22005

Published by Peter Lang GmbH, Berlin, Deutschland

info@peterlang.com - www.peterlang.com

This publication has been peer reviewed.
www.peterlang.com

Contents

Introduction

"You cannot serve both God and Mammon." (Mt 6:24)

It is difficult to imagine human life without money. It is said that "money rules the world." It is omnipresent. Money has been and continues to be a phenomenon that not only forms the foundation of economic life, an essential dimension of human existence, but also influences personal and familial life, shapes social relationships, impacts political life and culture, and enables technological development, including medical progress. It saves lives but also leads to disputes and wars.

The task and mission of the Catholic Church are to accompany people on their earthly pilgrimage toward eternal life. Furthermore, it is the People of God who are the subject of this earthly pilgrimage. Every person, whether Christian or non-Christian, undertakes the daily effort to subdue the land (Gen 1:28). Everyone constantly struggles with daily joys and worries. Some of them involve money, that is, the effort to earn it and satisfy needs through it. Therefore, it seems natural that the Catholic Church should have a clear stance on money. The first source of the Church's teaching is Holy Scripture. At first glance, the Church's attitude toward money appears to be negative, leading to a well-known statement from the Gospel of Matthew: "You cannot serve both God and Mammon" (Mt 6:24). However, a deeper reflection on the Bible reveals that the topic of money is much broader. Money-related topics found in the Holy Scriptures include wealth and prosperity, wages and salaries, inheritances, savings, investments, financial planning, taxes, tariffs, contributions, donations and sacrifices, bankruptcy, and debts, temptation by money, wealth related to securing human life. Furthermore, as Bauer notes, Jesus himself speaks more about money than heaven and hell.[1]

So, the Church should have much to say on the subject of money. Therefore, two questions seem justified: (1) What is the Catholic Church's stance on money? And (2) How does the Church understand money? An attempt to answer these questions is the subject of this work.

It is surprising that the topic of money itself only sporadically appears in the literature on the social doctrine of the Church. There seems to be no single book

1 Cf. Bauer (2006, p. 15). For more on money in the Bible, see, e.g., Stryczek (2015, pp. 16–116). A collection of biblical references to money with brief explanations can be found, e.g., in Johnson (2011).

in the German-language field of Catholic social doctrine dedicated to this topic. The book by Nell-Breuning–Müller,[2] which includes "money" in its title, falls within the realm of economics. The same applies to a section on money in the works of Schwindt[3] and a section in the work of Strzeszewski.[4] In the vast majority of publications on Catholic social science, the term "money" not only does not appear in the title but also is absent as a separate chapter or section or not even present in the index. However, this does not mean that literature does not address money-related themes, such as wealth and poverty. Money itself is rarely the subject of investigation.

This work will be divided into three main chapters. The first two will serve as a starting point and background for the analyses presented in Chapter 3.

These questions must be clarified from the beginning. The research topic will by no means be money in general but money in the sense of the Church's social doctrine. The Church is a multidimensional reality. Catholic social doctrine is one dimension of the Church's mission, with "this world" as its immediate subject. The first chapter of this work will, therefore, deal with the approach to the Church's social doctrine. It will be a starting point that prepares the ground and outlines a framework for further considerations. In this sense, analyses of money in other areas of Church teaching, such as the Old and New Testaments or the tradition of the Church, and the practice of handling money in the Church, go beyond the research framework chosen here.

Catholic social doctrine is based on two foundations: on the one hand, on Scripture and Tradition, and on the other hand, on the observation of reality, including the use of the achievements of modern science. When assessing the Catholic Church's stance on money, it seems justified to consider this question in a broader context. Therefore, the second chapter will provide a brief overview of the understanding of money in contemporary scientific disciplines. Since economics has the most to say about money, the starting point will be the presentation of the understanding of money in this scientific discipline and then in other disciplines such as sociology, psychology, ethics, and the contemporary specific approach known as the theology of money.

In the third chapter, attempts will be made to find answers to the research questions raised. On the one hand, the work of broadly understood Catholic social thinking is extremely rich, and on the other hand, there is an authoritative

2 Nell-Breuning (1962).
3 Schwindt (2015, pp. 88–93).
4 Strzeszewski (2003, pp. 92–97).

teaching within the Church. Therefore, the research will focus on the statements of the Church's teaching. However, due to the enormous number of such statements by the Church, the research will focus on the most important papal documents, which constitute the canon of social doctrine and are not limited to particular churches. Specifically, the attempt to answer the research questions will be based on an analysis of contemporary social doctrine of the Church, contained in the papal encyclicals from Leo XIII's "Rerum Novarum" to Pope Francis's "Fratelli Tutti."

The analysis of papal teaching will be based primarily on the texts available on the Holy See's website (www.vatican.va). However, in order to better understand the content of the popes' thought, the study of the encyclicals will be based on their published official translations in four languages: English, Latin, German and Polish.[5]

---

5 Unless specifically noted, translations of citations from literature in other languages into English are the author's.

1. Catholic Social Doctrine

1.1. The Church's Social Thought as Part of the Church's Mission

According to Catholic Church teaching, the rule of Jesus Christ expresses itself in three types of ministries: the prophetic, priestly, and kingly. The Church is the Body of Christ, and as such, it participates in these three forms of ministry. In the life of the Church, they manifest themselves in the proclamation of the Word of God, the celebration of the sacraments, and pastoral care.[1]

The social thought of the Church (Catholic Social Doctrine) emerged from the encounter of the joyful message of Christ, especially the requirements of the commandment of love of God and neighbor and the principle of justice, with the problems of the world.[2] Pope Benedict XVI defines Catholic Social Doctrine with the following words: "It is 'caritas in veritate in re sociali': the proclamation of the truth of Christ's love in society."[3] And elsewhere: "Love is the principal path of the Church's social doctrine (*Caritas praecipua est Ecclesiae socialis doctrinae semita*)". Every responsibility and obligation described in this teaching arises from love, which, according to the words of Jesus, summarizes the entire law (cf. Mt 22:36–40)."[4] The proclamation and dissemination of Social Doctrine are part of the Church's mission of evangelization, which, in turn, is an aspect of its prophetic dimension. More precisely, Catholic Social Doctrine is one of the elements of the so-called New Evangelization.[5] According to Pope John Paul II, the Church's Social Doctrine reveals the direct consequences of the Christian message for social life and is an element of Christian testimony. This means, in particular, that it is impossible to address fundamental social issues without reference to the Gospel.[6] However, the official Social Doctrine of the Church is not only directed at its members but also at all people of good will and even, without

1 Cf. Katholische Kirche (1985, pp. 211–214, 275–276).
2 Congregation for the Doctrine of the Faith (1986, no. 72).
3 Benedict XVI (2009, no. 5).
4 Benedict XVI (2009, no. 2).
5 The New Evangelization aims to find new ways and approaches to proclaiming the Gospel in Western countries that have undergone a process of secularization. See Vatican Radio (2010).
6 Cf. John Paul II (1991, no. 5).

exception, to all people.[7] The Pope understands the Social Doctrine of the Catholic Church as one of the expressions of the Church's social concern, that is, concern for authentic human and societal development, which means respecting and promoting the human person in all dimensions.[8] In this context, it is a particular concern of the Church to (1) create the necessary space for fulfilling its mission in the world and (2) for the dignity of individuals and peoples, including the manifestation of evil and injustice. In the second area, the Church emphasizes that the deepest sources for addressing social problems must be sought at the moral level, not only regarding temporal but also transcendent human vocation. Therefore, the Church's task is not to propose concrete solutions in the field of economic or political life but rather general statements of a religious and moral nature that provide a framework for discussing the problem and understanding what, from the Church's perspective, constitutes its essence.[9] John Paul II emphasizes that the Social Doctrine of the Church is an independent category from existing economic systems, especially capitalism and Marxist collectivism, and cannot be seen as a kind of "third way." It is also not an ideology. To quote the Pope, it is "the accurate formulation of the results of a careful reflection on the complex realities of human existence, in society and in the international order, in the light of faith and of the Church's tradition."[10]

The terms "Social Doctrine" and "Social Teaching" are used interchangeably, with the former referring to the historical and practical dimension and the latter to the theoretical dimension of the Church's teaching on social issues.[11] In scholarly literature, a distinction is also made between Catholic Social Teaching, Catholic Social Thought, and Catholic Social Ethics.[12]

The term "social teaching" refers to the statements of the Church's Magisterium.[13] Statements of the Church's Magisterium on social issues contain

---

7 Cf. John XXIII (1963, no. 91); John Paul II (1987, no. 47); Vatican Council II (1965b, no. 2).

8 John Paul II (1987, no. 1).

9 Cf. Himes (2005a, pp. 5–6).

10 John Paul II (1987, no. 41).

11 Cf. Guidelines for the study and teaching of the Church's Social Doctrine in the formation of Priests (1998, no. 1). Himes claims that John Paul II practically used the terms "Social Teaching," "Social Doctrine," and "Social Magisterium" synonymously. Cf. Himes (2005a, p. 4).

12 Cf. Gaillardetz (2005, pp. 86–87).

13 The expression "disciplina socialis catholica" comes from Pope Pius XI (1931a). Subsequent popes took up this term. For more, see Pontifical Council for Justice and Peace (2006, no. 87).

normative content, and they are characterized by a more conservative approach, representing an attempt to articulate a broader consensus within the Church. Therefore, they often avoid controversial and, as claimed by Gaillardetz, prophetic positions of individual representatives of Catholic social thought. Furthermore, this teaching is not connected to a scientific paradigm in the social sciences and the results of these sciences since it would be difficult to formulate normative statements based on the achievements of these sciences, which are inherently not absolute but socially and methodologically conditioned.[14] Catholic social thought, on the other hand, includes the statements of the Magisterium as well as texts by Catholic writers, thinkers, institutions, or others expressing their views on social issues from a perspective of faith.[15] More precisely, the sources of Catholic Social Doctrine can be distinguished into: (1) sources of revelation, that is, the Holy Scripture and the tradition of the early Church; (2) documents of councils and synods; (3) pastoral documents of popes and bishops, especially individual and collective (e.g., from bishops' conferences) pastoral letters of bishops and pastoral documents of the Holy See, especially the written pronouncements of popes, such as encyclicals or apostolic letters; (4) the achievements of Catholic scholars, especially theologians, philosophers, sociologists, and economists, with the first three belonging to Catholic Social Doctrine in the strict sense.[16]

The Social Doctrine differs from Social Ethics in terms of goals and methods. The former aims to explain, inspire, and guide moral reform in social matters, with the Church's voice being less methodical and more pastoral. Social Ethics deals with the description of reality (in the descriptive part) and the specification of laws and ethical norms (in the normative part) based on critical, systematic, and scientific research.[17]

Contemporary Catholic Social Doctrine, what is now referred to as Catholic Social Teaching, began with the encyclical "Rerum novarum." Since that

---

14 Cf. Gaillardetz (2005, p. 87).

15 Neuhold, referring to Zsifkovits, identifies Catholic social thought with a broadly understood Catholic social doctrine. In his view, the latter can be defined as "a teaching derived from the Catholic faith or at least not in contradiction with the Catholic faith, set forth in documents of the Church's Magisterium and oriented toward the occasion, and represented in Catholic 'schools' or advocated by important Catholic authors, concerning the social, with the term 'social' here understood in the broad sense of the word" (Zsifkovits, 1990, p. 16). In: Neuhold (2000, p. 15).

16 Cf. Majka (1986, pp. 10–12).

17 Cf. Himes (2005a, pp. 3–4). However, John Paul II locates Catholic social teaching within moral theology. Cf. John Paul II (1987, no. 41).

time and building on the fundamental ideas laid out by Pope Leo XIII in this encyclical, successive popes have deepened and developed the social theme in the context of their times, primarily through the Magisterium of the Bishops of Rome. These statements constitute the updated doctrinal corpus, the teaching structure of the Magisterium.[18] The so-called Social Encyclicals have become the most important form of communication for conveying the Church's social doctrine.[19] Roos divides them into two groups: Social Encyclicals in the strict and broader sense. The first group consists of the aforementioned encyclical "Rerum novarum" (1891) by Pope Leo XIII and encyclicals published on the occasion of their round anniversaries (in chronological order): "Quadragesimo anno" (1931) by Pope Pius XI, "Mater et magistra" (1961) by Pope John XXIII, "Laborem exercens" (1981) by Pope John Paul II, "Centesimus annus" (1991) by Pope John Paul II. This group also includes "Mit brennender Sorge" (1937) by Pope Pius XI, "Divini redemptoris" (1937) by Pope Pius XI, "Pacem in terris" (1963) by Pope John XXIII, "Populorum progressio" (1967) by Pope Paul VI, "Sollicitudo rei socialis" (1987) by Pope John Paul II, "Caritas in Veritate" (2009) by Pope Benedict XVI, "Laudato si'" (2015), and "Fratelli tutti" (2020) by Pope Francis. In the broader sense, the Church's social documents also include not only other encyclicals, such as the encyclical "Deus Caritas est" (2005) by Pope Benedict XVI or the encyclical "Spe salvi" (2005) by the same pope, but also, among others, the Pastoral Constitution "Gaudium et Spes" (1965) of the Second Vatican Council (1965), the Apostolic Letter "Octogesima adveniens" (1971) by Pope Paul VI, the Apostolic Exhortation "Evangelii nuntiandi" (1975) by Pope Paul VI, the Apostolic Exhortation "Evangelii Gaudium" (2013) by Pope Francis, and the declaration of the Synod of Bishops "De iustitia in mundo" (1971).[20] This catalog also includes radio addresses and Christmas messages, especially from Pope Pius XII during World War II.[21]

18 Cf. John Paul II (1987, no. 1).

19 An encyclical, in general, is a printed statement of the Pope in the form of a circular letter "addressed to the entire episcopate of the Church or to a part of it and, through it, to the faithful or to all people of good will" and has content related to "matters of faith and morals, philosophy, and social, state, and economic teachings, as well as discipline and church policy." It serves as a tool for the exercise of the ordinary universal magisterium and is the most important form of papal proclamation. See May (2017, cols. 697–698).

20 Cf. Roos (2008, pp. 125–126).

21 Cf. Majka (1996, p. 38).

Among the authors who engage with the Church's Social Doctrine, there is no consensus on the universally accepted canon of Catholic Social Teaching. There is no dispute over the most important social texts, but disagreements concern two areas: 1. There is no complete consensus on the subject of Catholic Social Doctrine, particularly the question of whether the teaching on marriage and family—and thus, church documents on this topic—belong to the Church's social doctrine or not (e.g., the encyclical "Humanae vitae" by Paul VI). 2. The fact that not all texts remain timeless, and some documents have lost significance over time (e.g., Pius XI's encyclical "Divini redemptoris").[22]

1.2. The Essence of Social Doctrine

It is the task of the Church to constantly seek the truth, tirelessly proclaim it, and understand it. Catholic Social Doctrine is and has never been conceived as a closed and complete system; instead, it is a continually updated response of the Church in dialogue with humanity and the world. It is knowledge illuminated by faith, meaning faith and reason are two sources from which it draws. In this sense, the Church's Social Doctrine belongs to the field of theology.[23] The social teaching of the Church derives from Sacred Scripture and the tradition of the Church. In them, it seeks and finds God's plan for humanity and the world, that is, human dignity as God's creation, as a person, and the vocation to trinitarian communion with God, with other people, and with the world.

The collaboration of faith and reason within Catholic Social Doctrine takes place on at least two levels. First, it seeks to understand God's plan through reason and comprehend its practical consequences. Second, it is open to the truth coming from various sources of knowledge and various scientific disciplines.[24] The Church's teaching is understood as a factor that unites these partial truths (i.e., it allows them, along with faith, theology, and metaphysics, to find their place within the framework of cooperation that serves humanity) and conveys them in the life of societies and peoples.[25] Thus, two characteristic features of this teaching are continuity and renewal. On the one hand, it is based on

22 Cf. Himes (2005a, pp. 4–5).

23 More precisely, the Catholic Church understands its social teaching as part of moral theology; that is, its doctrinal framework also includes moral judgments. Cf. *Catechism of the Catholic Church* (2003, nos. 2420, 2422).

24 Cf. John Paul II (1991, no. 59).

25 Cf. Benedict XVI (2009, nos. 9, 31). For more, see, e.g., Pontifical Council for Justice and Peace (2006, nos. 76–78).

fundamental, universal values derived from revelation and human nature. On the other hand, it is in constant dialogue with the ever-changing world.[26]

At this point, it is necessary to draw attention to another important dimension of the Church's Social Doctrine. It is not a purely theoretical teaching since it is part of the Church's evangelizing mission, it has a pastoral dimension. This applies to all the Church's statements on social issues, including those contained in encyclicals. Encyclicals are neither technical documents for solving specific problems nor scientific dissertations in the strict sense. They are authored by popes who, while often being significant theologians like Benedict XVI, are primarily shepherds. Therefore, the documents they publish on matters of church doctrine are essentially pastoral and should be treated as such.[27]

In summary, the Social Doctrine of the Church has three important dimensions: a theoretical one, a historical one, and a practical one. It is a teaching that seeks to establish an organic and systematic connection to reality based on universally valid principles. It relates to reality in its historical dimension, meaning it seeks to provide answers to the problems of the world that arise throughout history. It is an impulse and a call for a practical response *hic et nunc*.[28]

1.3. Methodology of Teaching

With Pope John XXIII, there comes a change and clarification in the methodology of the Social Doctrine of the Church. John XXIII not only abandons an abstract, a priori approach to the subject matter and adopts a pragmatic approach based on dialogue and cooperation, but he also proposes a new methodology for Catholic Social Doctrine.[29] In "Mater et Magistra," John XXIII introduces three stages for implementing the principles of Catholic Social Doctrine, which he names as: look, judge, act.[30] These are: (1) review of the actual situation, (2) assessment of the situation in the light of the principles of natural law and Christian teaching, (3) determination of the possibility of implementing the principles of the Church's Social Doctrine.[31]

---

26 Cf. Pontifical Council for Justice and Peace (2006, no. 85).

27 Cf. Nitecki (2010, p. 201).

28 Cf. Congregation for Catholic Education (1998, no. 6).

29 This method can be classified as a dynamic inductive-deductive approach. Cf. Congregation for Catholic Education (1998, no. 7).

30 This method, developed by Joseph Cardijn, is described as a three-step approach. Cf. Mich (2005a, pp. 196–198)

31 Cf. John XXIII (1961, no. 236).

To delve into these points further: The first step involves understanding and investigating the real problems and their causes. Here, modern science can contribute significantly, making cooperation and dialogue with it necessary. However, the Catholic Social Doctrine cannot uncritically and thoughtlessly accept or receive the results of individual scientific disciplines, especially in the social sciences. It is necessary to be able to make a careful distinction, even with the help of the right philosophical perspective. Otherwise, there is a risk that the Social Doctrine of the Church will not build its theses on truths that are in harmony with right reason, Christian faith, and well-founded scientific knowledge but on pseudo-truths rooted in ideologies.[32]

In the assessment phase, it is essential to confront what has been observed with the sources of the Social Doctrine of the Church. Here, the teaching authority of the Church plays the most crucial role. Its task is to interpret reality through the prism of faith and provide guidance, counsel, and impulses to humanity and society.

The third step can be summarized in the Christian call "Repent, and believe in the Gospel" (Mk 1:15). The purpose of the Social Doctrine of the Church is not only to show people the right way of life in this world from the perspective of the Catholic faith but also to lead them to salvation.

1.4. Constituent Elements of Catholic Social Doctrine

The essence of Catholic Social Doctrine consists of three constituent elements that are inseparably linked to the methodology applied by this doctrine. These elements are the enduring principles, criteria for evaluation, and guidelines for action.

The social principles are the "building laws" and cornerstones of the social moral order.[33] They are unchanging and universally applicable principles and instruments through which the Church can address individual and societal problems and challenges. They also serve as the starting point for creating alternative responses and solutions to existing ones.[34] They encompass the following principles, which can be divided into two groups: those related to human understanding and those concerning the foundations of societal life. The first group includes the principle of the human person, the principle of freedom, and the

---

32 Cf. Congregation for Catholic Education (1998, no. 10).
33 Cf. Weiler (1991, p. 36).
34 Cf. Corkery (2007, p. 69).

principle of the interdependence of individuals and society, while the second group includes the common good principle, subsidiarity principle, participation principle (participation), solidarity principle, and the principle of the universal destination of goods.[35]

The starting point and central fundamental principle of Catholic Social Doctrine is the concept of the human person. The human being is understood here as a being endowed with reason and free will, and therefore a subject of rights and duties.[36] The human person has inherent dignity because they are created in the image and likeness of God and destined for eternal life. In the human person, the entire creation finds its pinnacle, center, and reference point. In the context of the personalistic approach to the individual, it is essential to remember that they are both a sinful and a redeemed being. Therefore, great emphasis is placed on the inner and outer freedom of the individual. The Second Vatican Council formulates the principle of freedom as follows: "(…) man's dignity demands that he act according to a knowing and free choice that is personally motivated and prompted from within, not under blind internal impulse nor by mere external pressure."[37] However, the human being cannot be understood as a closed monad. By nature, they are a social being, one whose natural habitat is to have relationships with others. The human being cannot be self-sufficient, and detached from society, they are incapable of full development. On the other hand, it is impossible to conceive of a society without individuals who make it up and who contribute to its existence, development, and diversity through their talents and calling. Therefore, the principle of interdependence between the human being and society is one of the foundations of the Social Doctrine of the Church.

In addition to the above-mentioned principles, Catholic Social Doctrine also reveals the fundamental values that should guide human life because they result from human dignity. These values include truth, freedom, justice, and love. Only when these values are lived can a person find the right path to personal development and the construction of a more humane society.[38]

The most important principle in societal life is the principle of the common good. It is the highest law of society.[39] This rule is to be understood such that, under otherwise equal conditions, the well-being of the individual is subordinated

---

35 Cf. Congregation for Catholic Education (1998, no. 36).
36 Cf. Congregation for Catholic Education (1998, no. 31).
37 Vatican Council II (1965b, no. 17).
38 Cf. Pontifical Council for Justice and Peace (2006, nos. 197–208).
39 Cf. Weiler (1991, p. 37).

to the common good, with the aim of enabling both groups and their individual members a more complete and easier achievement of their fulfillment.[40] Thus, the common good aims at recognizing and promoting the human dignity of all. The other principles serve to create a society in which the common good can be realized. According to the principle of participation, every person who is a member of a community has the duty and right to participate justly, adequately, and responsibly in the development of its socio-economic, political, and cultural life. This is the only way to achieve the common good and the fullness of human development.

The principle of subsidiarity was defined by Pope Pius XI. It states: "Just as it is gravely wrong to take from individuals what they can accomplish by their own initiative and industry and give it to the community, so also it is an injustice and at the same time a grave evil and disturbance of right order to assign to a greater and higher association what lesser and subordinate organizations can do. For every social activity ought of its very nature to furnish help to the members of the body social, and never destroy and absorb them."[41]

It is a principle that determines the structure on which the reality between the different components of society should be based. It emphasizes the importance of federalism and decentralization, understood as the primacy of one's own actions, rights, and responsibilities over support from other actors, especially those higher up in the social structure.

The principle of solidarity draws attention to the commitment each person has toward society because it has created the conditions for their life and development and has passed on culture, scientific and technological knowledge, as well as material and immaterial goods. This principle is a prerequisite and a call to engagement for the common good and for overcoming and transforming the structures of sin into structures of solidarity.[42] Pope John Paul II synthetically formulated the principle of solidarity, stating that "we are all really responsible for all."[43]

The principle of the universal destination of earthly goods arises directly from God's creation. God has destined the earth and everything it contains for the benefit of all people and nations; therefore, these created goods must benefit everyone in fair proportion. Thus, the human being, who uses these goods

---

40 Cf. Vatican Council II (1965b, no. 26).

41 Pius XI (1931b, no. 79).

42 Cf. Pontifical Council for Justice and Peace (2006, nos. 193–195).

43 John Paul II (1987, no. 38).

legitimately, should regard external things not only as personal property but also as common goods, in the sense that they can be useful not only to themself but also to others.[44] This principle should not be ideologically interpreted, meaning that the Church is placed in a position where it negates private property (as in communism). The Church not only accepts the right to private property but also defends it. However, it does not absolutize it but relativizes it by emphasizing the social function of property.

In the Social Doctrine of the Church, it is not just about general principles, but since its purpose is practical, namely the conversion and moral renewal of humanity, the Church's social documents also include an evaluation of reality. This assessment arises from the right and duty of the Church to make moral judgments. The criteria for such evaluation are based on the foundation of Scripture and Tradition and must consider both local and global conditions, including cultural, social, political, and economic aspects. The specific purpose of such judgments is to help the faithful recognize their vocation in the world correctly and make decisions and actions in accordance with the spirit of the Gospel.[45] Some of the guidelines are only directional for the faithful, but there are also statements from the Church that are binding.[46]

1.5. The Social Teaching of the Church Before the Encyclical "Rerum novarum"

Due to the fact that the primary source of Catholic Social Doctrine is revelation, the brief historical overview of this doctrine should begin by highlighting the ideas and social institutions found in the Bible. For Christians, the source of revelation is the entire Holy Scripture, meaning both the Old and New Testaments.

1.5.1. The Old Testament

The idea contained in the early pages of the Old Testament is the concept of the creation of humanity as *imago Dei* (Genesis 1:27). Man, created in the image and likeness of God, shares responsibility for the entire creation. He has the right not only to develop the Earth, including the use of its resources, but also to improve it. However, this image is supplemented by the teaching of the fall of man

---

44 Cf. Vatican Council II (1965b, no. 69).

45 See Congregation for Catholic Education (1998, nos. 47–64). Examples of such judgments can be found in section 1.6 of this book.

46 See section 1.7 of this book.

(Genesis 3:1–4:16) and God's will and continuous effort to restore the covenant with humanity, especially with the chosen people (Exodus 24:1–11).

The Old Testament also contains the principle of the primacy of divine natural law over secular law, human law (Isaiah 10:1–2). The ideas and norms found in the Old Testament serve as a normative framework for the construction of political systems and social institutions, such as property (God is the owner of the promised land), the duty to share the gifts of the land with other members of the chosen people, the duty to help the poor (Deuteronomy 15:7–9), including the obligation to give tithes (Deuteronomy 26:12) or alms (Tobit 4:17), the condemnation of greed and the pursuit of excessive wealth (Isaiah 5:8). In the pages of the Old Testament, you can also find regulations concerning labor protection (Leviticus 25:43) and fair wages for work (Jeremiah 22:13). Furthermore, there are also regulations regarding usury or certain forms of social assistance and social security (e.g., Leviticus 25:35–38).[47]

1.5.2. The New Testament

Similar to the Old Testament, the New Testament cannot be reduced solely to its social dimension, but it is also impossible to ignore this dimension. The social teaching of the New Testament can be divided into the teachings of Christ and the teachings of the apostles. Christ does not reject the law of the Old Testament, nor does He replace it with new laws; instead, He reveals and teaches what the true law is, which simultaneously fulfills the law of the Old Testament. This can be summarized in His words: "Be perfect, therefore, as your heavenly Father is perfect" (Matthew 5:48). This perfection of God is manifested in His love, which is why the commandment to love God and neighbor is emphasized above all in the New Testament (Matthew 22:37–40).[48] This commandment is primarily a call to change an individual's attitude. It is an appeal to prioritize spiritual values over material ones (Matthew 6:33). Christ outlines the path to achieving this goal in the Sermon on the Mount, emphasizing the tools (Matthew 5:3–12). Only a new, transformed person is capable of changing the society in which they live.

47 Cf. Majka (1986, pp. 25–42).

48 Love should not be understood as the abolition of justice because love is the fulfillment of the law or justice (Rom 13:10).

Among Christ's teachings, there are also statements related to specific economic issues.[49] The first beatitude in the Sermon on the Mount (Matthew 5:3) is not an encouragement for poverty in the economic sense. It is an encouragement not to be attached to the goods of this world, not to accumulate wealth at any cost, and to practice generosity, helping others, and showing kindness. The encouragement not to worry about worldly matters (Matthew 6:25–34) is not meant to detach people from worldly concerns like the necessity to work but to redirect their attention to higher values, with worldly matters being only instruments for this purpose. Furthermore, Christ did not condemn property or money. Regarding property, He sometimes recommended renunciation as a path to perfection (Matthew 19:21), but He also spent time among the wealthy (Luke 19:1–10). His disciples possessed money, sometimes in large sums (Mark 6:37).[50] The issue of work is also present in the life and teachings of Jesus. He was the son of a carpenter, and in His parables, He praised those who were diligent and resourceful (Luke 16:1–8, 11–12).[51] A breakthrough in Jesus' teaching is His message that all are chosen by God for salvation, that all are one people who can turn to God the Father (Luke 11:2–4), and thus, all are equal before God. This statement has important consequences for social life. It can be a prerequisite for the creation of a society based on democratic principles. It also introduces a new family model with equal rights for all members, especially for women and children.

The other books of the New Testament contain both the teachings of the apostles, which are an interpretation of Christ's teachings, and practical descriptions and guidelines for the life and work of the early Christian communities.[52] The first challenge facing early Christianity is the question of the universality of Christ's message. The decisions of the so-called Council of Jerusalem opened the Church to all people (Acts 15:22–29). Importantly, this universal message is not seen as contradictory to patriotism. Paul, the apostle to the Gentiles, does not hide his Jewish patriotism (Acts 28:20). Another social issue confronting the

49 Majka maintains that Jesus' statements on economic issues should be interpreted with caution and, in particular, should not be of a purely economic nature, but the rules for economic life should be derived from them. Cf. Majka (1986, pp. 56–57).

50 In this passage, it is said that the disciples had 200 denarii. A denarius at that time was roughly equivalent to a day's wage of a laborer. See Lau (2013, pp. 7–8).

51 Cf. Stryczek (2015, pp. 28–30).

52 Majka claims that it is possible to look for a method for solving social problems among the apostles, although it is necessary to take into account the social and civilizational context of that time. Cf. Majka (1986, p. 59).

Church at that time is political power. Similar to the Old Testament, it is believed here that power comes from God, and its purpose is found in that belief (Romans 13:1). However, power itself cannot be deified because those who wield it do not come directly from God but should exercise the entrusted power in the spirit of serving the common good and protecting society from evil (Romans 13:4). While experience shows that power can be abused, early Christianity does not call for revolution but rather for witnessing in such a world as the one they live in (Romans 13:7). In other words, the concept of the two powers, the spiritual and the secular, derived from Christ's words, "My kingdom does not belong to this world" (John 18:36), slowly takes shape in the early Church. One of the features of the early Church was communal sharing of goods (Acts 2:44). Renunciation of property in the Christian community, however, was not an obligation but a form of charity stemming from the commandment of love and the recommendation to assist the poor (Acts 5:1–11).[53] The author of the Letter to the Ephesians describes greed as idolatry, raising the question of whether the New Testament condemns money and wealth for this reason (Ephesians 5:5). The answer to this question is provided in the First Letter to Timothy (1 Timothy 6:9–10). The evil does not lie in things themselves but in people's attitudes toward them. It is greed for money and the desire for wealth that lead to many temptations and entanglements, enslaving people. People have the right to possess temporal goods, but they are only truly free when they share and use them for good (2 Corinthians 8:11–15). In this context, it is understandable that members of the Christian community were encouraged to work for profit so that the money earned could be shared with the needy (cf. Ephesians 4:28). Furthermore, it is emphasized that it is the employer's duty to pay fair wages (James 5:4).[54]

1.5.3. Church Fathers

The social teaching in the tradition of the Church can generally be divided into the teachings of the Church Fathers, especially with the contribution of Saint Augustine, the teachings in the Middle Ages with the central position of Saint Thomas Aquinas, and the teachings in modern times, primarily represented by the Social Doctrine of the Scholastics.

The statements of the Church Fathers are usually homiletic. Although they are not the central focus, social topics find expression in their teachings due to

---

53 Starting with the word *communio*, Rodziński calls this social order "communionism." Cf. Rodziński (1960, p. 104).

54 Cf. Majka (1986, pp. 59–74).

their proximity to the daily lives of Christians. The most frequently addressed social issues by early Christian authors include: duties related to property, acts of mercy, work, wealth, poverty, almsgiving, usury, and in subsequent times, the question of the Christian model of the state also emerges. Despite the radical nature of some of these statements, they should not be taken as a call for revolution but rather as a call for a change of heart. Social questions can be found in writings such as the Epistle of Barnabas, the Shepherd of Hermas, the Didache, and among the following authors: Tertullian, Saint Clement of Alexandria, Saint Athanasius, Saint Basil the Great, Saint John Chrysostom, Saint Ambrose, Saint Jerome.

1.5.4. Aurelius Augustine

The most significant author of the patristic era was Aurelius Augustine, who was the first to attempt to create a concept of the Christian state. Among many of his statements, "De Civitate Dei" holds a central place in this topic.[55] Although Saint Augustine does not present a complete socio-economic and political system, the foundations of such a system can be found in his teachings. The background for this work was the invasion and plunder of Rome by the Visigoths in the year 410.

Augustine distinguishes between two types of cities/states: the earthly (*civitas terrena*) and the divine (*civitas Dei*). He refers to the former as Jerusalem and the latter as Babylon. The origins of these cities are two types of love. At the end of Book XIV, Augustine describes them as follows: "What we see, then, is that two societies have issued from two kinds of love. Worldly society has flowered from a selfish love which dared to despise even God, whereas the communion of saints is rooted in a love of God that is ready to trample on self. In a word, this latter relies on the Lord, whereas the other boasts that it can get along by itself. The city of man seeks the praise of men, whereas the height of glory for the other is to hear God in the witness of conscience."[56]

The second type of love is Christian and oriented toward the common good and the preservation of peace, but it does not exclude justice, while the first is guided by egoism, selfishness, and the desire for conquest.

When Augustine describes the history of humanity, he sees it as a struggle between good and evil that will continue until the end of time.[57] However, his

55 Höffe refers to it as the most important book of Christian philosophy of the state and philosophy of justice. Cf. Höffe (2006, p. 77).

56 Saint Augustine (2008b, bk. XIV, chapter 28).

57 Cf. Saint Augustine (2008a, bk. I, chapter 35).

concept should not be limited to a purely political message. For him, this struggle takes place more within the individual, and only the individual's inner decision for one of these worlds has political and social consequences.

1.5.5. Thomas Aquinas

Among the medieval thinkers who delved into social issues were Saint Thomas Aquinas, Saint Bonaventure with his concept of a social order based on the hierarchy of angels (*hierarchia coelestis*), and John Duns Scotus, who considered the state as a community of communities (*communitas communitatum*) and is viewed by some commentators as a precursor to the concept of the social contract. However, the most significant of them was Saint Thomas Aquinas.[58] His rich literary output also includes three works directly addressing social issues.[59] However, understanding his ethical, political, and social views necessitates reference to his major works like the "Summa Theologica" and the "Summa Contra Gentiles," among others. Thomas's main idea is to demonstrate the interconnections between the four orders of being and thought, that is, the physical, metaphysical, moral, and supernatural.

According to Aquinas, God's plan for managing the world is contained in the eternal law (*lex aeterna*). This law consists in imparting God's wisdom to all that God has created. Human beings, as rational creatures, are gifted to participate in the eternal law, what Thomas calls the natural law (*lex naturalis*). The natural law derives from the eternal law and allows a person to recognize by reason what is good and what is evil. The third and last level is human-made law, which, in order to be "law," must conform to divine law and natural law. The purpose of law is for created beings to achieve a certain perfection of existence, understood as participation in the Good and manifested through action. This striving for perfection, as understood in this way, is a particular command for human beings as moral agents capable of moral progress. It involves conscious action with a hierarchy of goals, including the ultimate goal of human life (*finis ultimus*), which is God. It also implies an order and hierarchy in the world, including the political and social sphere, with God at the pinnacle. This order is based on the principle of justice (*ordo iustitiae*), which reflects and partakes in God's justice (*iustitia divina*). The person is an elemental subject of social life, inherently a social

58 The reconstruction of St. Thomas's views presented here is based on Majka (1986, pp. 112–131).

59 These are: De emptione et venditione ad tempus, De regimine Iudeorum ad ducissam Brabantiae und De regimine principium ad regem Cypri.

being. Through their actions, individuals create a society, which is a system of persons in mutual relations striving for the common good (*bonum commune*). As the realization of the common good is a prerequisite for the realization of individual good (*bonum privatum*), it takes precedence over the latter. Thomas regards the family and the state as fundamental natural communities. He views the state as a *societas perfecta*, a self-sufficient, independent, and self-governing community ruled by an authority (the ruler). The ruler's role involves legislating and enforcing the law, as well as ensuring external peace and satisfying the temporal needs of the citizens.

One dimension of social life is economic activity. Thomas incorporated many economic ideas from Aristotle, including the division of goods into natural goods, which satisfy needs, and artificial goods, including money, which facilitates exchange since all other goods can be purchased with it. However, it's not possible to simply reduce Thomas's thoughts to imitating Aristotle's views. Saint Thomas asserts that the pursuit of economic activity and wealth is natural and good for humans. Yet, this should also be considered within the hierarchy of goals. Neglecting this hierarchy makes it difficult or impossible to attain higher goals. This means that economic goods, while inherently good, are merely means to achieve other goals, including the ultimate one. They enable the attainment of higher goals in three ways: they ensure survival, allow for good deeds, and provide an adequate social status.

In the context of economic goods, the question of property is significant. Saint Thomas affirms private property but makes two critical distinctions: (1) between the owner (*dominus rei*) and the possessor (*possessor rei*), and (2) between the right to property and the right to use. The right to property arises from human rational nature, enabling individuals to manage and dispose of things in ways that serve others and contribute to the common good. Thomas thus emphasizes the social function of property. The right to use, on the other hand, arises directly from the right to life and is an essential part of natural law, belonging to every person. In other words, not everyone can lawfully possess material goods, but everyone has the right to use them for individual and common well-being. One relevant observation here is that Thomas accepts and justifies the right to property but also emphasizes that private forms of ownership result from original sin, as before sin, there was only a form of co-ownership.

Another vital question raised by Saint Thomas Aquinas is that of the fair or just price and value of economic goods. When analyzing the value of things, Thomas points to both objective factors (e.g., production costs) and subjective factors (e.g., buyer preferences). This combination of factors determines the price of a particular good on the market. However, two principles of exchange are crucial here. Firstly, it must be mutually advantageous, and secondly, it must occur at a fair price, meaning a price that ensures equality of advantages for both participants in the exchange. What is the prerequisite for such equality? According to Saint Thomas, the measure of exchange cannot be subjective, particularly not based on need, as profiting from another's need for one's advantage is nothing other than usury.[60] Therefore, the only possible objective measure is the effort and costs required to produce a particular good.

1.5.6. The School of Salamanca

The doctrine of Saint Thomas provided the foundation for the development of Catholic teachings in the centuries that followed. Notable among these developments is the so-called Spanish Scholasticism, which contributed to the revival of Saint Thomas's thinking in the 16th and 17th centuries. Its founder was Francisco de Vitoria, who taught at the University of Salamanca and is thus considered the founder of the School of Salamanca. Other representatives of this school included Domingo de Soto, Martín de Azpilcueta, Tomás de Mercado, Juan de Medina, Luis de Molina, Juan de Mariana, and Francisco Suárez.

Among the key views advocated by de Vitoria were those related to international law and war. According to de Vitoria, the state is a natural institution willed by God. Starting from the premise that humans are inherently social beings, Francisco de Vitoria also introduced the concept of a global community that includes all humanity. The law governing relations between states is referred to as international law (*ius inter gentes*). Secondly, de Vitoria believed that war, in general, is an evil but allows for it as a last resort (*ultima ratio*). The laws of war, as presented by de Vitoria, permit defensive war and, in certain cases, even preemptive war, limited to the restoration of damage caused by the enemy when all peaceful means have been exhausted.[61]

The reflections of the authors of the School of Salamanca were not confined to legal and political matters. They also made significant contributions to Christian thought on economic issues, focusing primarily on the ethical and legal framework for the functioning of the market.[62] Topics of particular interest to them included private property and trade, fair price and subjective value theory, usury

60 An overview of Thomas Aquinas' theory of interest is presented in Chapter 2.

61 Cf. Bruch (1980, pp. 3263–3266).

62 They tried to describe and understand the surrounding reality, which was subject to profound changes. In their works, they did what is considered the first stage in the contemporary methodology of Catholic social teaching, which is called "looking."

and interest rates, banking theories, monetary theory, inflation, taxation, and public finance.[63] It's worth mentioning Martín de Azpilcueta, who is considered the first to outline the basics of what is known as quantitative monetary theory.[64]

Closely related to money is the issue of its devaluation and inflation. One of the main critics of the state's inflationary policies through the destruction of the value of money was Juan de Mariana. He pointed out the economic, social, and political consequences of such policies. He believed that the devaluation of money by the ruling authority was, in fact, a tax or even theft, ultimately threatening the entire state.[65]

One of the most significant achievements of the School of Salamanca was the formulation of a subjective theory of value and the associated price theory. The value of goods primarily depends on their appraisal (*aestimatio*) by the buyer, meaning that in commercial transactions, this subjective factor is the primary consideration.[66] In this context, it is worth noting that Luis de Molina argued that the value of money, in addition to its quantity, also depends on subjective factors, meaning its fluctuations are determined by human estimation.[67]

1.5.7. Encyclicals before "Rerum Novarum"

With Benedict XIV, encyclicals were introduced as a new instrument for conveying the teachings of the popes in the Catholic Church. Before Leo XIII, nine predecessors issued a total of 77 encyclicals.[68] Among the topics addressed in these encyclicals is the response to the actions of rulers and states that interfere in religious matters, oppress citizens, and even resort to violence against them. Specific issues raised by the popes included the expulsion of the Jesuits, the establishment of state-controlled religious structures, and anticlerical actions following the French Revolution. In their encyclicals, the popes protested against the confiscation of land and church property, the destruction of charitable and

---

63 Cf. Alves & Moreira (2013, pp. 65–85).

64 Cf. Azpilcueta (2004, sec. 51). According to the quantity theory, the value of money depends on its amount in the market.

65 Cf. Alves & Moreira (2013, pp. 82–83).

66 Cf. Majka (1986, p. 151).

67 Cf. Molina (2015, p. 96).

68 Schuck categorizes these encyclicals chronologically into: encyclicals published before the French Revolution; encyclicals from the time between the French Revolution and the coronation of Napoleon; and encyclicals from the time after the Napoleonic Wars up to Leo XIII. Cf. Schuck (1991, p. 1).

educational institutions, the dissolution of religious communities, and the lack of respect for Catholics in the realms of religion, politics, family, economy, and culture.

Regarding economic matters, the popes of that time focused on two main themes: unethical business practices and theft. Unfair conduct by merchants (including Jews), resulting in excessive profits from trade, fraud, Sunday work, and usury, was part of the first group. Concerning theft, the popes intensified their criticism of liberal states and socialism. They not only highlighted theft, especially the theft of property, but also advocated for private property. Cultural matters within the papal sphere of interest included concerns and criticisms about the proliferation of books, freedom of speech, the secularization of education, and moral issues like alcohol consumption and the spread of prostitution.[69]

The teachings of the popes are not merely a critique of reality; they also propose solutions that combine a theological perspective with social recommendations. Their starting point is the biblical image of the shepherd and his flock, where the world is seen as a pasture. The metaphor of the pasture is significant because it can be considered a place that provides sustenance and rest, but it also contains wolves, including wolves in sheep's clothing. In this context, it is the shepherd's duty to teach the sheep, that is, to show what is good and to warn against evil. As for social recommendations, they can be applied to the five dimensions of human life: religious, political, familial, economic, and cultural.

From a religious perspective, the popes emphasize the unity of the Church. They point to the organizational unity of the Catholic Church as a whole and its activities in the areas of evangelization and education, including seminary, priestly, and theological education, as well as the spiritual renewal of the clergy and the laity. In the dimension of political life, the popes' observations concern the origin, purpose, and exercise of state authority, citizenship, the relationship between church and state, political freedoms, and rights. The popes remind that all power comes from God, and rulers are servants of God who should ensure public safety and the equality of rights. The divine origin of authority also implies the duty of citizens to obey authorities acting justly, but they also have the right to disobey when laws enacted by authority contradict divine law.

Regarding the relationship between the state and the Church, the popes address three specific questions: the separation of church and state, areas of shared jurisdiction, and the social and institutional primacy of the Church as a *societas*

69 Cf. Schuck (1991, pp. 1–11).

perfecta. The popes also provide theological justification for human rights and civil liberties, deriving them from God's law.

In the realm of family life, the popes address three groups of issues: the nature and purpose of marriage, the proper relationship between spouses, and the responsibilities of spouses and parents. They borrow from Augustine's understanding of marriage the concept of procreation and education of children as the primary purposes (Augustine calls them primary goods) of marriage. At the same time, they emphasize the second of these purposes, namely the education of children, and point out that the education of children in God and religion is the fundamental duty and purpose of marriage.

In the field of economic life, the teaching of the popes concerns the participation of Christians, including in business management, in the emerging market economy. The Church affirms the involvement of the faithful in business activities, including the investment of funds in business enterprises and, to a limited extent, in loans and other financial transactions (such as currency exchange). This presupposes private property, including real estate, which is also accepted by the popes, albeit with the reservation that property should not be understood as absolute.

Regarding the relationships between the poor and the rich, the popes' position is not uniform. On one hand, they propose a model of complementarity that acknowledges differences in ownership but emphasizes the harmonious coexistence of the poor and the rich, with both groups being able to give something to each other. The rich should help the materially poor, and in return, the latter should show gratitude and obedience to the former (this is the position of Pius IX). On the other hand, for instance, Clement XIII calls on all Christians to practice restraint, renounce their possessions, and be content with what they receive, namely food and shelter. In this context, almsgiving is not seen as an expression of generosity but as a matter of justice.

Finally, concerning the last, that is, the cultural dimension of societal life, the popes of the pre-Leonine era advocate for joint church and state censorship of books, monitoring of education, and the fight against secret societies, especially Freemasonry and socialism.[70]

---

70 Cf. Schuck (1991, pp. 19–31).

1.6. The Main Themes of Modern Catholic Social Teaching

The beginning of modern Catholic social teaching can be traced back to the encyclical "Rerum Novarum" in 1891. Although, as shown, Pope Leo XIII's encyclical was not the starting point of the Church's teachings on social issues, it did mark a "new path" and a "fresh start" for addressing social matters. This particular encyclical initiated and inspired the ever-increasing and more comprehensive involvement of the Church in social issues. Therefore, in literature on this subject, when referring to "Catholic social teaching," particular emphasis is placed on the teachings of the popes that were initiated by this encyclical of Leo XIII.

Scholarly literature presents the Church's social teaching in at least two ways. Some authors analyze individual papal documents, usually in chronological order.[71] Others attempt to systematize papal teachings by themes.[72] Here, we adopt the second perspective and use the "Compendium of the Social Doctrine of the Church," published by the Pontifical Council for Justice and Peace, as the basis for analysis.[73] This choice is made because it is an official document of the Holy See that summarizes the social doctrine of the Church. The Compendium covers the following themes: the family, human work, economic life, the political community, the international community, the protection of the environment, and the promotion of peace.[74]

1.6.1. The Family

The Catholic Church emphasizes that the family is the first natural community with its own rights. These rights take precedence over other forms of society (i.e., society and the state) and, therefore, place the family at the center of societal life. The family is crucial for the formation of a person as an individual and as a subject of social life. Above all, individuals learn in the family what love is and what community in the sense of "communio" means.[75] For this reason, society

71 This group includes, e.g., Himes (2005b); Nell-Breuning (1977); Strzeszewski (2003).

72 Examples of this group include Curran (2002) and Klose (1979).

73 Pontifical Council for Justice and Peace (2006).

74 Cf. Pontifical Council for Justice and Peace (2006, nos. 209–520). Himes believes that other issues such as racism, nationalism, antisemitism, feminism, institutional self-critique of the Church, and how the Church's institutional self-interest can shape its teachings on social issues are not adequately addressed by the Church. Cf. Himes (2005a, pp. 5–6).

75 The term "communio" has central significance in the Catholic Church because it describes the relationship between the three divine persons. See Drumm (2017).

and the state should prioritize the family in their societal models and support it in fulfilling its duties according to the principle of subsidiarity.

At the core of the family is the marriage between a man and a woman. The significance of this relationship is evident from the fact that it holds the status of a sacrament. However, the family does not consist only of the spouses; it also includes their offspring and the elderly ("community of generations"). Each person within such a family has their dignity and place.[76]

The family plays a role in shaping societal life, including economic life. On one hand, for many people, their home is the center of economic activity, and, importantly, families are guided less by market logic and more by principles of sharing and mutual solidarity. On the other hand, families and their members, as employees or employers, form the institutions of economic life. In this context, work, wages, and property are of great significance. Work not only enables the establishment of a family but also its sustenance. Through work, both the employee and their family have opportunities for development. The Catholic Church believes that work should be compensated with a just wage, known as the (family) living wage.[77]

1.6.2. Human Labor

Human labor is neither a punishment nor a curse. However, after the original sin, it can sometimes bring hardship and suffering to people. This doesn't mean that work itself is bad. Work is a duty of humans, but it is not the meaning of their life. It is merely a tool and a means to achieve the goal of human life, which, from a temporal perspective, is the integral development of the individual and, from an eternal perspective, is God. Through work, humans become collaborators with God in the work of creation. Through work, people can participate in the fight against poverty and strive to achieve dignified living conditions and even prosperity. But this should not be an end in itself, nor should it be elevated above the value of the human being. This is why the right to rest on holidays is emphasized.[78]

---

76 The Charter of Family Rights states in the preamble that "the family is the place where different generations come together and help one another to grow in human wisdom and to harmonize the rights of individuals with other demands of social life." The Holy See (1983, no. F).

77 Cf. Vatican Council II (1965b, no. 67).

78 With the social changes of the nineteenth century came the so-called "*worker question*, that is, the problem of the exploitation of workers brought about by the new industrial organization of labour, capitalistically oriented, and the problem, no less serious, of

The necessity for the Church to address this issue became a premise for the encyclical "Rerum novarum." From that point on, the issue of labor, framed within the context of the social question, became a constant theme in the Pope's social doctrine. The Church's teaching here focuses on presenting a personalistic view of labor and continuously reminding people of this perspective.

Human labor can be considered in two dimensions: a subjective one and an objective one. It is the person, in their actions (*actus personae*), who is the subject of labor. Work in this subjective sense is an inherent part of human nature. The fact that a person is the subject of work gives it a particular dignity and does not allow it to be reduced merely to a narrowly defined commodity or an element of production organization. The dignity of human work, therefore, arises from the dignity of the human person performing it.[79]

Work in the objective sense encompasses all the activities a person engages in and the resources they use in their work, such as tools, techniques, and resources employed during work. This understanding of work is transient because it changes with technological, organizational, cultural, social, or political developments. Human labor also has a social dimension, which means that it is carried out with and for others; with others because of the organizational aspect of work, which increasingly requires cooperation, and for others because the fruits of labor often do not solely satisfy one's own needs but become objects of exchange.[80]

Human labor is not limited to interpersonal relationships but extends to relationships with the factors of production, especially capital. Here, the Catholic Church's position is clear. Since the person is the subject of work, everything else, including capital, should be subordinated to them. This applies particularly to capital. This does not mean an opposition between labor and capital or a conflict between them but rather a hierarchy within complementarity. In the social doctrine of the Church, capital can be understood in various ways. Typically, the term refers to material means of production, although in early encyclicals, the terms "labor" and "capital" were related to two social classes.[81] Later encyclicals

---

ideological manipulation—socialist and communist—of the just claims advanced by the world of labour." Pontifical Council for Justice and Peace (2006, no. 267).

79 John Paul II states that "human work has an ethical value of its own, which clearly and directly remain linked to the fact that the one who carries it out is a person" (1981, no. 6).

80 Cf. John Paul II (1991, no. 43).

81 Cf. Leo XIII (1891b, no. 15).

began to emphasize that, in a sense, the person is capital too—their skills, experience, and so forth are essential for work.[82]

In the context of the relationship between labor and capital, the issue of private property is essential. Based on the principle of the universal destination of goods, the Church advocates for the right to property. Concerning employees, this implies two demands: first, that employees can be co-owners of enterprises, including having influence on their management. It is crucial that property serves the purpose of work.[83] Second, there is a demand for work that allows employees not only to provide for themselves and their families but also to save money and increase their wealth.[84]

The Church is aware of many labor-related issues and doubts that these problems can be solved without the involvement of the state. Therefore, the role of the state and civil society is to promote the right to work and labor protection. In particular, it is the duty of the state to create conditions for full employment. However, this cannot be achieved through the suppression of individual initiative or rigid regulations that discipline economic life. In the context of globalization, political action should not only focus on national affairs but also involve international cooperation.

1.6.3. Economic Life

Christianity views economic life and economic activity as a response to God's Old Testament call from the Garden of Eden for humans to cultivate and care for the garden (Genesis 2:15) and the New Testament command for humans to develop their talents (Matthew 25:14–30). The Church believes that "(...) man is the source, the center, and the purpose of all economic and social life."[85] The Church sees a close connection between the moral law and economic laws, which is why its social doctrine focuses on the moral aspects of economic life. Moral norms, by their nature, are general and reveal the highest and ultimate purpose of human life, enabling the establishment of a hierarchy of goals and assigning a place for economic goals within that hierarchy.[86] In this way, economic goals, including production, distribution, and consumption, can lead to

82 Cf. John Paul II (1991, no. 32).
83 Cf. John Paul II (1981, no. 14).
84 Cf. Leo XIII (1891b, no. 4).
85 Vatican Council II (1965b, no. 63).
86 Cf. Pius XI (1931b, pp. 42–43).

the holistic development of individuals and humanity as a whole, becoming a space for salvation and sanctification.

The development of talents would not be possible without economic freedom and initiative. Through them, a person, as an individual and creative subject, can realize themselves, and the dimension of human life that is entrepreneurship becomes a reality.[87] In the social doctrine of the Church, the economy is understood in an organic manner. It consists of individuals who perform various functions in economic life. Some are employees, others are entrepreneurs, and some are capital providers, among others. They all form a single socio-economic organism made up of various smaller units, with businesses being the most important among them. A business is understood as a solidarity community that should serve the common good of society by providing goods (and services) to that society. When considering entrepreneurship, Catholic social doctrine highlights several themes. Firstly, profit is seen as an expression of a company's proper functioning. However, this profit should not be achieved at the expense of the dignity of the people working in the company. Secondly, it is emphasized that a company's activities should not be limited to the economic dimension but should also be seen in the social dimension. A business should contribute to the development of individuals and society, with a particular focus on promoting the family.

Economic life can also be examined from a broader perspective, raising questions about the proper use of resources. This is important because there is a widespread belief that resources are limited while human needs are unlimited. In other words, Catholic social doctrine must address the scarcity of resources and the boundless nature of human needs. In this context, the Church's statements focus on the role of institutions such as the market or the state in the service of humanity.

The Catholic social doctrine not only does not reject the free market but affirms it and appreciates its advantages: "*A truly competitive market is an effective instrument for attaining important objectives of justice*: moderating the excessive profits of individual businesses, responding to consumers' demands, bringing about a more efficient use and conservation of resources, rewarding entrepreneurship and innovation, making information available so that it is really possible to compare and purchase products in an atmosphere of healthy competition."[88]

87 Cf. John Paul II (1987, no. 15).
88 Pontifical Council for Justice and Peace (2006, no. 347).

Of course, this does not mean that the Church's attitude toward the market is uncritical. As in the entire economic sphere, it is necessary to place the economic dimension on a moral foundation. It is essential to be aware of the limitations of the market, especially its narrow view of the human being and society and its inability to satisfy all human needs solely based on market mechanisms. In this regard, it seems understandable that the Catholic Church attributes significant importance to the state alongside the market. The first role of the state is to define the legal framework that should regulate economic life. Secondly, the state should define and direct economic development. The state can also engage in active public policies, including the use of public finance instruments such as taxes or social benefits.[89] In this case, it is essential that the state is guided solely by the common good and acts based on the principles of subsidiarity and solidarity.

Specific economic issues addressed by Catholic social doctrine at the national level include topics such as (a) consumption, emphasizing that it cannot be an end in itself; (b) wealth, highlighting its role as a servant of individuals and society; (c) nonprofit organizations, which may offer a different understanding of economic issues compared to market enterprises and enrich the economic organism.

There is also the highest level of economic life, which concerns the planet as a whole and, in economic terms, globalization and international economic and financial relations. The Church is not afraid of globalization but acknowledges its negative consequences (e.g., the relative enrichment of rich countries and the impoverishment of poor countries). Therefore, the Church calls for support to the poorest regions and the creation of equal market conditions for all countries participating in international trade. In the modern world, the international financial system, including financial markets, plays a significant role. The Church warns against the detachment of the financial sector from the real economy and against financial crises. The stability of the financial system is a prerequisite for stable economic development and, consequently, for the comprehensive and solidary development of humanity.

1.6.4. The Political Community

Christianity considers humans not only as social beings but also as political beings. This implies that the existence of a political community is justified by human nature. A political structure can only function well if it makes the

89 Cf. Vatican Council II (1965b, no. 30).

centrality of the human person its foundation.[90] This also means that the human person is and must be both the subject and the goal of all social institutions.[91] The immediate consequence is that the political community, in its pursuit of the common good, must be based on moral principles and protect and promote fundamental and inalienable human rights. This also means that the political community, in its pursuit of the common good, must be based on moral principles and protect and promote the fundamental and inalienable human rights. It should do this by creating "a human environment," that is, by establishing conditions under which citizens can exercise their human rights and fulfill the associated duties.[92] From the Church's perspective, the deepest and fullest expression of this is the evangelical commandment of love.

The Church believes that the political community truly expresses itself in a people.[93] A people is a political structure whose members are characterized by a community of life and values. However, this does not mean that a people is understood as a single nation. Members of the same people may also be representatives of other nations, that is, ethnic minorities, who should have laws in place for their protection.

A political community is a derivative of civil society. The compendium defines civil society as "(…) the sum of relationships and resources, cultural and associative, that are relatively independent from the political sphere and the economic sector."[94] Civil society is therefore a space in which citizens can enter into a variety of relationships to find solutions to meet their basic needs, defend their legitimate interests, and build a just social life.

The personalistic foundation of civil society also implies the nature of political authority. The Church has never advocated anarchy; on the contrary, it has pointed out the need for legitimate power. The Church understands authority as a quality of persons or institutions that are authorized to issue laws and orders to people, and people should adhere to them.[95] However, it must do this in the spirit of service and based on the principles of solidarity, subsidiarity, and justice.

Authority is of divine origin and, like the political community, is based on human nature. This does not automatically mean that every power, in and of

---

90 Cf. Congregation for the Doctrine of the Faith (2002, no. 3).

91 Cf. Vatican Council II (1965b, no. 25).

92 Cf. Pontifical Council for Justice and Peace (2006, no. 389).

93 Cf. Pius XII (1944, sec. I).

94 Pontifical Council for Justice and Peace (2006, no. 417).

95 Cf. *Catechism of the Catholic Church* (2003, no. 1897).

itself, is legitimate. It is only legitimate when its decisions are oriented toward the common good, and it uses morally acceptable means to achieve this goal.[96] Otherwise, a citizen is not bound by conscience to obey such an authority. Furthermore, they are obliged to refuse participation in the activities of the morally evil.[97] Natural law and divine law take absolute precedence over positive law.

Regarding specific systemic solutions, the Church sees democracy as the best form to enable citizens' participation in political life.[98] However, a democratic system is not a value in itself. It requires the rule of law and a correct understanding of the human person.[99] Depriving democracy of these elements and basing it on ethical relativism is one of the greatest threats to this system. Among the many specific issues of political life addressed by Catholic social doctrine, the question of religious freedom and the independence of the state from the Church holds a special place. The Church stands for the right to freedom of conscience and religion.[100] At the same time, the Catholic Church expects the state to respect autonomy and independence, including the creation of the space necessary for unhindered action. The Church, in turn, acknowledges that specific political issues, including political agendas, do not fall within its sphere of interest unless they relate to religion and morality. Therefore, the Church does not take on the role of a commentator on current political issues. However, this does not preclude cooperation between both institutions, as both serve the human being.

1.6.5. The International Community

The Christian message is a proposal for all of humanity because it presents a universal vision of man and the world, with its temporal and ultimate goal being the unity of the human community.[101] The international community is the organizational form and the tool to achieve this goal here on Earth. The Catholic Church understands it as a legal community in which international relations should be based on the principles of mutual aid and freedom understood as sovereignty, which excludes unjustified interference in the internal affairs of other countries and any oppression of one country by another.[102] However, sovereignty is not

---

96 Cf. *Catechism of the Catholic Church* (2003, nos. 1902–1903).

97 As an example of such morally evil actions that require resistance, John Paul II mentions abortion and euthanasia. Cf. John Paul II (1995, no. 73).

98 Cf. Congregation for the Doctrine of the Faith (2002, no. 3).

99 Cf. John Paul II (1991, no. 46).

100 Cf. Vatican Council II (1965a, nos. 1–8).

101 Cf. Vatican Council II (1965a, no. 1).

102 Cf. John XXIII (1963, no. 120).

an absolute value for the Catholic Church. Based on the personalistic principle, the Church's social doctrine takes the position that the establishment of an international community should focus on the human person and the common good of all people. For this reason, it must be based on the same values that are essential for creating bonds between people, namely truth, justice, love, and freedom.[103] For this reason, nations can freely limit their sovereignty to make it easier to achieve the common good. It is essential to refer to universal principles that transcend individual states' domestic laws when building an international community, as relying solely on positive law can risk violence becoming an instrument in international relations. The Church emphasizes that there are universal principles that stand above the domestic law of individual states and must be considered in formulating international law.[104] These principles include the obligation to honor agreements (*pacta sunt servanda*), the rejection of war as a means of conflict resolution, the duty to cooperate for the common good, and the equal dignity of every nation.

The demand for the common good on an international level concretely means cooperation to guarantee the right to the integral development of every person and every nation. Since the holistic development of the individual is a right, it is the duty of societal structures, from the smallest to the international community, to do everything in their power to guarantee this right and enable its realization. This necessitates collective action and mutual assistance on various levels, including the economic, political, social, medical, educational, and especially the fight against poverty.

It is self-evident that individual states must be involved in building the international community, but that is not sufficient. The Catholic Church emphasizes the role of international organizations such as the United Nations, international movements, and its own role, advocating the creation of a kind of global authority whose task would be to ensure international peace and security, the respect for justice, and the protection of rights.[105]

1.6.6. Preservation of the Environment

The pastoral constitution "Gaudium et spes" underscores the value of human creativity. It follows the directive given by God that humans should have dominion over the Earth (Genesis 1:26–28). By creating humans in His own image

103 Cf. John XXIII (1963, no. 167).
104 Cf. John Paul II (2004a, no. 5).
105 Cf. Vatican Council II (1965b, no. 82).

and likeness, God has allowed them to participate in the work of creation. Thus, human activity is a part of God's own work. However, for this to be realized, people must acknowledge that it is not they but God who is the Creator in the original sense. Consequently, men must govern the world in which they live "with justice and holiness" and relate everything to God, so that God's name may be praised at all times and in all places.[106] From this perspective, human creativity acquires its value. This applies to all areas of human activity, including science and technology. This view, however, demands that human actions must not destroy the work of creation and, therefore, God's plan. In particular, humans must not endanger the environment.

At the beginning of the 21st century, the ecological question became a central point in the Church's social doctrine. Any human activity that harms Sister Earth or our common home contradicts God's plan.[107] Such actions prioritize the self-interest of some over human intentions and, in doing so, eliminate God's intentions.[108] Humans become tyrants who manipulate and exploit nature and its resources, contributing to its degradation, which in turn harms humans themselves. On the other hand, the Church opposes the concept of biocentrism or ecocentrism, ideologies that treat humans only as a part of nature and thus strip them of their dignity and responsibility within the work of creation. An integral ecology, which aims for comprehensive environmental protection and treats it as an economic, political, social, cultural, and moral challenge, is a task for all of humanity.[109]

1.6.7. Promotion of Peace

The last of the major areas addressed by the Church's social doctrine is the promotion of peace. The Church has the duty to proclaim the message of peace and work for peace, as this is part of its proclamation of the Gospel.[110] The source of peace is God Himself. Therefore, peace and its propagation are not only a value but also a universal obligation.[111] Peace involves the abstention from violence, especially from war. It is not only about seeking alternative ways to resolve conflicts.[112] International organizations like the United Nations and the

106 Cf. Vatican Council II (1965b, no. 34).
107 Cf. Pope Francis (2015, nos. 2, 13).
108 Cf. John Paul II (1991, p. 37).
109 Cf. Pope Francis (2015, nos. 138–162).
110 The Gospel is the good news of peace. (Eph 6:15).
111 Cf. Paul VI (1969).
112 Cf. John XXIII (1963, no. 67).

International Court of Justice can also play a crucial role in maintaining world peace. In special cases, however, the Church allows for necessary defense, including the use of military force. But the Church understands peace as more than just the absence of war. Peace springs from a personalistic view of humanity and requires the continuous establishment of a just and loving order. From this, the emphasis on protecting the civilian population, caring for refugees, and advocating for the rights of ethnic, religious, or linguistic minorities derives. It also includes the condemnation of terrorism and the consistent call for disarmament, particularly the elimination of arsenals of weapons of mass destruction. According to the Church, no effort for peace can succeed without prayer, mutual forgiveness, and reconciliation. The annual World Peace Days, which began on January 1, 1968, are a concrete expression of this conviction.[113]

1.7. The Binding Nature of Catholic Teaching on Social Issues

1.7.1. Catholic Social Teaching as the Teaching of the Whole Church

The third book of the Code of Canon Law, which deals with the Church's ministry of proclamation, begins with a clear statement: "It belongs to the Church always and everywhere to announce moral principles, even about the social order, and to render judgment concerning any human affairs insofar as the fundamental rights of the human person or the salvation of souls requires it."[114] From this, it follows that the Church's social doctrine is the teaching of the entire Catholic Church. It is an expression of how the entire Church perceives social matters. The task of developing and teaching it belongs to every member of the Catholic Church. Naturally, each contributes according to their vocation. This contribution is also manifested in the supernatural sense of faith of the entire people and in paying attention to the signs of the times.

So, what is the contribution of each member of the Church in creating and implementing social doctrine? It is crucial to distinguish between the universal prophetic mission of all the baptized and the official teaching.[115] The Magisterium in the Catholic Church can be defined as follows: "Magisterium, Magisterium of the Church (Latin 'magisterium', since the 19th century), within the

113 Cf. Paul VI (1968).
114 Code of Canon Law (1983, canon 747 §2).
115 Cf. Aymans (2015, p. 912).

community of the Church, it is the testimony instance of the Christian faith, whose bearers (individual bishop, collegial bishop bodies, Pope) are directly authorized by virtue of sacramental ordination (hence, 'Magisterium') to present, with binding authority, the contents of divine revelation for faith and life, and indirectly to decide on safeguarding statements related to it, in cases of dissent."[116] The Magisterium of the Church has the task of preparing and teaching the social doctrine of the Church. In particular, it is the task of the Pope and the Council to set the direction and determine the development of this teaching. At the same time, it is the task of the bishops, on the one hand, to stimulate the Magisterium of the Pope through suggestions and, on the other hand, to explain this teaching and apply it to the specific situation of their respective dioceses. The task of clergy and laity is to shape the social doctrine in accordance with their charismas and to apply it in their daily lives.[117]

What does this mean exactly? How should a Christian's response to the teaching of the Church's Magisterium in social matters be? Christians should not view the Church's teaching as a series of piecemeal instructions, each requiring a specific kind of approval. Instead, they should, in the spirit of following Christ, do their best to ensure that the Gospel is put into practice and thus proclaimed.[118] At this point, the question of the relationship between the Magisterium and the other members of the Church is relevant. Above all, the question arises to what extent the faithful are bound by the statements of the Church's Magisterium.

First, it must be said that the Church warns the faithful against a know-it-all attitude: "Whoever believes they are entitled to have a better understanding of the Church's future insight than the current teaching of the Church must, in sober self-critical evaluation before God and their conscience, ask themselves

116 "Lehramt, kirchliches Lehramt (lat. *magisterium*, seit dem 19. Jh.), ist innerhalb der Gemeinschaft der Kirche jene Bezeugungsinstanz des christlichen Glaubens, deren Träger (Einzel-Bischof, kollegiale Bischofs-Gremien, Papst) aufgrund der sakramentalen Ordination (daher: Lehr-"Amt") direkt die Inhalte der göttlichen Offenbarung für Glaube und Leben, indirekt die damit verbundenen Sicherungsaussagen authentisch, d. h. mit verbindlicher Autorität, vorzutragen und bei Dissens darüber zu entscheiden befugt sind" (Beinert, 2017, col. 751). The word "magisterium" comes from the Latin magister, which means, among others, president, chief, director, superintendent, etc., and in ecclesiastical Latin, teacher. The noun magisterium refers to the office of a magister, so in church terminology it means the office of a teacher or teaching office.

117 Cf. Pontifical Council for Justice and Peace (2006, nos. 79–80).

118 Cf. Gaillardetz (2005, p. 87).

whether they possess the necessary breadth and depth of theological expertise to deviate from the current teaching of the Church in their private theory and practice. Such a case is fundamentally conceivable. However, subjective arrogance and hasty know-it-all attitudes will have to answer before God's judgment."[119] However, this does not mean that every statement of the Church should be understood dogmatically.

Not every utterance of the Church's Magisterium has the same binding force on the faithful, so we can speak of a so-called graded binding nature.[120] To make it clear, the Magisterium of the Church can be characterized by describing it through the following questions, which simultaneously serve as criteria for distinguishing various aspects of the Church's teaching: What are the contents of the teaching? Who exercises this teaching? Is the teaching addressed to the entire Church or a particular part of it? What forms does the teaching take?

1.7.2. Definitive and Other Binding Doctrines of Faith

Canon law reaffirms and codifies that the task of proclaiming the Gospel and the authority of the Magisterium in the Church belong to the Pope and the college of bishops.[121] Regarding the content of the doctrine, a distinction can be made between the definitive doctrines of faith in the Church and other binding doctrines of faith.[122] Concerning the former, the Code of Canon Law distinguishes between truths formally revealed by God and entrusted to the Church and truths of faith and morals that indirectly derive from revelation.[123] It's important to differentiate between teachings that are endowed with infallibility and those that are not. Not all statements of the Pope or the college of bishops are infallible. However, this does not mean that such statements do not belong to the Magisterium.

---

119 "Wer glaubt, der privaten Meinung sein zu dürfen, die bessere künftige Einsicht der Kirche schon jetzt zu haben, der muß sich vor Gott und seinem Gewissen in nüchtern selbstkritischer Einschätzung fragen, ob er die nötige Weite und Tiefe theologischer Fachkenntnis habe, um in seiner privaten Theorie und Praxis von der augenblicklichen Lehre des kirchlichen Amtes abweichen zu dürfen. Ein solcher Fall ist grundsätzlich denkbar. Aber subjektive Überheblichkeit und voreilige Besserwisserei werden sich vor Gottes Gericht zu verantworten haben" (Döpfner, 1967, no. 19).

120 Cf. Deutsche Bischofskonferenz (1995, pp. 115–118).

121 Cf. Code of Canon Law (1983, canon 756 §1).

122 Cf. Aymans (2015).

123 Cf. Code of Canon Law (1983, canon 750).

Definitive doctrines of faith can be taught and communicated in various ways. In this context, we can speak of the extraordinary supreme Magisterium, also known as the solemn Magisterium, and the ordinary and universal supreme Magisterium.[124] The Bishop of Rome, by virtue of his office, possesses infallibility in teaching when he definitively and obligatorily (*ex cathedra*) proclaims doctrine concerning faith or morals.[125] The teaching of the college of bishops gathered at a council under the Pope's leadership is also infallible when it definitively proclaims doctrine concerning faith or morals, or when, though dispersed throughout the world, it unanimously expresses, in communion with the Pope, that a doctrine concerning faith or morals must be accepted as definitively valid.[126] It's crucial that a particular doctrine is considered infallible when it is clearly articulated as such.[127] The solemn Magisterium is, therefore, always expressed through a formal act (a formal act of definition). In contrast, the ordinary and universal supreme Magisterium is not in the hands of the Pope alone but depends on the communion of bishops with the Pope. It is not expressed through a formal collegial act but through the common faith and agreement of the faithful under the guidance of the Magisterium.[128]

Other doctrines of faith encompass any other doctrines proclaimed by the Church's Magisterium. However, these doctrines are not invested with a formal character of infallibility.

The faithful are obligated to assent to infallible truths proclaimed by the Magisterium (*assensus fidei*). In cases of non-infallible doctrine, the faithful should show religious obedience (*obsequium religiosum*) to this teaching.[129]

As for particular Churches or associations of particular Churches, the holders of the Magisterium are diocesan bishops or the collegiate episcopal bodies that are in communion with the Pope and the college of bishops (*communio hierarchica*). Although their teaching is not infallible, they are authentic teachers of the faith. Therefore, the faithful should show religious obedience to this teaching. Priests and deacons also participate in the official teaching ministry due to their ordination and mission as co-workers of the bishop.[130]

124 Cf. Code of Canon Law (1983, canon 750).
125 Cf. Code of Canon Law (1983, canon 749 §1).
126 Cf. Code of Canon Law (1983, canon 749 §2).
127 Cf. Code of Canon Law (1983, canon 749 §3).
128 Cf. Aymans (2015, pp. 913–915).
129 Cf. Riedel-Spangenberger (2017, p. 754).
130 Cf. Aymans (2015, pp. 916–918).

1.7.3. The Binding Nature of Catholic Social Doctrine

After these general remarks, the question of the binding status of Catholic Social Doctrine can now be addressed. Regarding the extent to which the Church's social teaching is binding for a Catholic, Gaillardetz suggests categorizing the statements of the Magisterium into three categories: (1) universal moral teachings (of a dogmatic nature), (2) specific moral principles, (3) the prudent application of specific moral principles.[131]

The first category includes the teachings that form the foundation of Catholic Social Doctrine and are valid in the conscience of every Catholic, even though they are not in the form of dogmas (the author refers to them as dogma, although they are not so in the formal sense). These teachings pertain to the law of love, the dignity of the human person, the respect for human life, and the duty to respect the environment.

The second category comprises the contents that result from the moral reflection of the Catholic Church in the light of theological and intellectual considerations, as well as rational reflection on human experience. These statements are conditionally binding, meaning they are not irrevocable. They do not bind Catholics in the same way as dogmas, but believers are still obliged to attempt to follow them, and they are authoritative in this sense. Examples of such statements include the affirmation of human rights in the political, social, and economic realms or the preferential option for the poor.

The last group consists of concrete applications of specific moral principles. This group includes, for example, the condemnation of the first use of an atomic bomb by American bishops. Believers should take these guidelines into account in their moral decision-making but also have the right to hold a different opinion.[132]

1.7.4. The Role of the Laity

The role of the laity in the Church's social teaching cannot only be seen from the perspective of their obedience to the Church's teaching but also through the prism of their participation in the threefold office of Christ.[133] In their priestly function, they are called to offer their entire lives and present them to God the Father with the sacrifice of the Lord's body in the Eucharist. Their prophetic

131 Cf. Gaillardetz (2005, pp. 89–90).
132 Cf. Gaillardetz (2005, pp. 89–90).
133 Cf. Vatican Council II (1964, no. 31).

mission means that they are called to bear witness to Christ in word and deed under the given circumstances of their lives. Finally, through their participation in the kingly office, the laity have received the gift of royal freedom, enabling them to renounce themselves, lead a holy life, and thereby overcome the dominion of sin within themselves and in the world.[134] The laity do not merely "belong to" the Church; they "are" the Church and, as such, have an important role in the world. The Second Vatican Council formulates their role as follows: "(…) the laity, by their very vocation, seek the kingdom of God by engaging in temporal affairs and by ordering them according to the plan of God. (..) Therefore, since they are tightly bound up in all types of temporal affairs it is their special task to order and to throw light upon these affairs in such a way that they may come into being and then continually increase according to Christ to the praise of the Creator and the Redeemer."[135]

A particular area of responsibility for the laity is to discover and seek means and ways to infuse the realms of social, political, and economic life with Christian faith and life. This task encompasses what is the subject of the Church's social teaching.[136]

134 Cf. Catechism of the Catholic Church (2003, nos. 901–913, 941–943).
135 Vatican Council II (1964, no. 31).
136 Cf. Catechism of the Catholic Church (2003, no. 899).

2. Money in Modern Sciences

2.1. Economics of Money

In general, modern economics is divided into microeconomics and macroeconomics. Microeconomics, in its simplest sense, deals with the analysis of the market and its participants.[1] On the other hand, macroeconomics focuses on the analysis of the entire economy, examining relationships between macroeconomic variables such as national income, total economic consumption, total economic investments, unemployment, inflation, business cycles, exchange rates, interest rates, and balance of payments. A significant area of macroeconomic research explores the effects of fiscal and monetary policies on the economy as a whole.[2] Since modern economics cannot be conceived without money, it falls within the purview of these two economic disciplines.

Within the framework of microeconomics, money is examined through the functions it can fulfill in the market. In macroeconomic considerations, however, money is analyzed through the lens of overall supply and demand, interest rates, exchange rates, and the actions of monetary and financial authorities. This leads to the examination of the following important points: (1) the functions that money can and does fulfill in the economy, (2) how modern money is created, meaning how it enters the economy, including the question of who issues and regulates the money supply, and (3) whether and what impact money has on the economy, including the question of the stability of the currency.[3]

2.1.1. The Origin of Money

Although the question of the origin of money has limited relevance for current economic considerations, it is still valuable to outline the main axis of the debate

---

1 Cf. Woeckener (2020, pp. 1–2).

2 Cf. Woll (2008, p. 505).

3 The system of modern money is understood here as the system that was created after the decision of the President of the United States, Richard Nixon, on August 15, 1971, to unilaterally withdraw the United States from the convertibility of the dollar into gold. This day is considered the end of the so-called Bretton Woods system. See Davies (2002, p. 523). In other words, modern money is understood here as money that is not connected to any commodity, especially not to precious metals. The supply of such money depends solely on the decision of the issuer.

on this topic, as this discussion has influenced the perception of money by other disciplines, such as sociology. In the economic-historical debate on the origin of money, two extreme positions can be distinguished. On one side are proponents of the idea of the market-driven origin of money, while on the other side are those who claim that money is the product of a political decision.

Advocates of the so-called convention theory of money argue that money spontaneously emerged in the market. One of the proponents of this position was Carl Menger, who believed that money is a spontaneous product of the free market and not an invention of the state. He wrote, "Money did not originate by law; it is, in its origin, a social, and not a state institution."[4] The state did not create money but merely recognized and regulated what emerged through market processes. Money appeared in the market because it facilitated the exchange of goods, enabling better satisfaction of needs.[5] In other words, the conventional theory of commodity money starts from the limitations of natural barter trade, which has two types of restrictions: subjective and objective.[6]

The first group of limitations relates to an individual's preferences when choosing to trade a good they have for something they need or want. Such a person must possess something they do not need themselves but are willing to exchange for the goods of another person. Additionally, the other party in the exchange must desire the same, meaning they want the goods of the first party while offering their own in exchange. There is also the issue of the so-called coincidence of wants, that is, how many goods should be exchanged for how many others.

The second group encompasses all restrictions concerning the place and time of exchange. Both parties to the exchange must meet, which is not always possible at the same time and place. Furthermore, the quality and durability of the goods to be exchanged pose a problem. Some goods can be stored for longer periods and do not need to be traded immediately, while others must be exchanged relatively quickly to retain their utility.

---

4 "Das Geld ist nicht durch Gesetz entstanden; es ist seinem Ursprunge nach keine staatliche, sondern eine gesellschaftliche Erscheinung" (Menger, 1936, p. 41).

5 Carl Menger is also considered the founder of the modern theory of money as a medium of exchange. See, e.g., Menger (1871, pp. 209–285).

6 According to Issing, historically, the origin of money should be sought in its use as a badge of rank, ornament, and sacred object. However, it seems that these two approaches are not contradictory, because commodity money was accepted because it also has a use-value in addition to its exchange value. Cf. Issing (2007, p. 1).

In such a system, money appears as an intermediary that facilitates or even enables this exchange. In this context, money in an economy can be defined as any commodity generally accepted in payment for goods and services or in settlement of other financial obligations.[7] The reason for this is that money can split the commodity exchange into two separate acts: (1) the sale of the held commodity for money and (2) the purchase of the desired commodity with money.[8] However, economic development was not only made possible by the appearance of money but also by the evolution of forms of money to adapt to new economic and civilizational conditions.[9]

In summary, it can be observed that money enabled market exchange by reducing information costs—all economic quantities (especially prices) are expressed in a unit, reducing transaction costs associated with exchanging goods and services—and it allowed for deferring purchases, thereby increasing the variety of possible consumption and investment decisions.

Supporters of an alternative approach to the origin of money argue that it is a product of the legal system. Knapp begins his work with the words, "Money is a creature of law; it has been created in the course of history in the most varied forms: a theory of money can therefore only be juridico-historical."[10] According to this approach, it was public authority that decided what money is, especially through the decision of what currency can be used to settle public-law obligations, particularly taxes.[11]

A somewhat different role of the state in relation to money is suggested by Heinsohn and Steiger, proponents of the so-called property theory of interest rates and money. According to their view, money is an anonymized property title and can only emerge in communities that sanction property rights.[12] In other words, the source of money is private property, to which the law gives public

7 Cf. Jarchow (2010, p. 1)

8 Nowadays, the type of economy in which money functions as a medium of exchange is referred to as a division of labor economy. This type of economy seems to contribute most effectively to economic development because it allows for high specialization and broad collaboration in the production and exchange process.

9 For more information on various historical forms of money, see, e.g., Davies (2002).

10 „Das Geld ist ein Geschöpf der Rechtsordnung; es ist im Laufe der Geschichte in den verschiedensten Formen aufgetreten: eine Theorie des Geldes kann daher nur rechtsgeschichtlich sein." Knapp (1918, p. 1). Knapp's approach is referred to as Chartalism.

11 See Wray (1998, p. 3). Larry Randall Wray is considered one of the prominent proponents of the so-called Neo-Chartalism, also known as Modern Money Theory.

12 Cf. Heinsohn & Steiger (2006, p. 97).

authority. The formal possession of property rights is a prerequisite for the possibility of encumbering this right by establishing a credit security. When credit is created, money is created.

Both streams of thought (market-oriented and state-oriented), even though they may appear contradictory, contain elements of truth and complementarity. It is true that money, especially the modern monetary system, is significantly influenced by political power. Still, it is also true that money fulfills certain functions in the market, and its forms change with economic and technological development.

2.1.2. Functions of Money

As mentioned earlier, proponents of the conventional theory of the origin of money emphasized its role, its function in market exchange. Therefore, money was defined in a functional manner, and the so-called functional approach to money was developed. John Hicks aptly put it: "[M]oney is defined by its functions: anything is money which is used as money: 'money is what money does.'"[13]

Traditionally, it was believed that money can serve three functions in economic life: the function as a medium of exchange (including a unit of account)—you pay with money, as a store of value—you save in money, as a unit of account (measure of value)—you count in money.[14] The first function, the function as a general medium of exchange, has already been discussed.[15] How does money fulfill the other two functions?

The mere fact that some time elapses between acquiring money and spending it means that, to be accepted as money, it must preserve its value. Although there are many other instruments for storing value (in modern economies, these can be bank deposits, stocks, artworks, for example), only money retains a constant nominal value and can be used as a means of payment at any time.

Money also possesses an abstract quality that is indispensable in a complex economy. As mentioned earlier, in a natural barter economy, there is a need to

---

13 Hicks (1967, p. 1).

14 Some authors distinguish four functions of money, i.e. they separate the function of a medium of exchange from that of a means of payment. In the first function, money acts as a mediator in the exchange of goods and services, and in the second, it serves as a means of settling debts. See Issing (2007, p. 1).

15 Many authors focus on this first function when defining money. An example of such a definition is given by Brudzinski: "Money is the universally accepted medium of exchange and payment agreed upon by a society." Budzinski (2018).

relate the value of one good to the value of another. Without a uniform unit of account, the relative value of goods would need to be determined directly. In an economy with n goods, the number of such interchangeable relationships is $n*(n-1)/2$, which is very complex. The emergence of money as a unit of account makes it a measure of the value of all goods, expressed in money, their price. Therefore, the price of such goods in an economy with n commodities is n-1 (money itself is not valued).[16]

While microeconomic definitions of money draw attention to its functions in the market, in macroeconomic terms, money relates to phenomena in the entire economy. From this perspective, it can be said that "money in the macroeconomic sense is a generally accepted and readily usable claim on the volume of goods and services (i.e., the social product) of an economy."[17] The characteristic of modern money is, therefore, the universality of its acceptance, which nowadays results from legal regulations and the fact that this money is essentially emitted in the form of credit.

2.1.3. Money Creation

In today's world, two forms of money can be distinguished: physical money and digital money. The first group includes cash (coins and banknotes), while the second consists of digital money, typically in the form of entries in accounts with the central bank or commercial banks.[18]

The modern currency system is structured in such a way that the primary producer of money is the central bank. It issues money by granting loans (including the acquisition of debt instruments) or, occasionally, by acquiring other financial assets on its own account. Such money creation by the central bank is reflected in the corresponding entries in its accounting system, especially in the accounts of those entities that have borrowed money from the central bank. When money is held in an account at the central bank, a specific entity (usually a commercial bank or the government) has the right to use it in two ways: either

16 Cf. Issing (2007, pp. 1–2).

17 "Geld im volkswirtschaftlichen Sinn eine allgemein anerkannte und jederzeit verwendbare Forderung auf das Güter- und Dienstevolumen (d.h. das Sozialprodukt) einer Volkswirtschaft ist" (Gerdesmeier, 2006, p. 3).

18 In addition to physical forms of money, there are also non-material forms of money, some of which are derived from the ones mentioned above (e.g., records on electronic information carriers, so-called electronic wallets), but do not possess the characteristics of universal acceptability (e.g., cryptocurrencies).

for cash withdrawal or for transfer to the account of another entity that also has an account with the central bank. In this context, the first quantitative definition of the money supply, which is used for conducting monetary policy, should be mentioned. Here, it is referred to as the M0 aggregate, which shows how much money has been issued by the central bank. Technically, M0 consists of currency in circulation and deposits of commercial banks with the central bank.[19]

The activities of commercial banks are licensed and strictly regulated because they are the primary "producers" of money for the economy, considering the money supply.[20] The money of commercial banks is transferred in the form of entries in their customers' accounts (demand deposits or various types of savings and time deposits).[21] The main source of money creation by commercial banks is lending to customers, which can be individuals, businesses, local governments, and public institutions, including the state.

At this point, we can discuss other quantitative definitions of money. This time, they answer the question of how much money is in the economy. Monetary aggregates can have various components and are individually defined by different central banks. However, it is important to note that an M1 aggregate includes money that is currently used as a medium of exchange and payment in the economy (generally, it includes cash circulating in the economy and digital money in customer accounts at commercial banks), while other aggregates (M2, M3, etc.) also include money as a store of value.

In summary, modern money is created as a result of credit activities within the banking system.[22] This has far-reaching implications for the form and structure of

---

19 Central bank money is sometimes referred to as "high-powered money" or "base money" because it forms the basis for money creation by commercial banks. See Gerdesmeier (2006, p. 16).

20 The term "commercial bank" here refers to all institutions (financial intermediaries) authorized to conduct banking activities, including granting loans and maintaining customer accounts in the form of deposits.

21 It is essential that the account holder has the right to convert the funds in their account into cash, i.e., central bank money. The condition for money issuance by commercial banks is, therefore, that they have access to central bank money. Hence, practically every commercial bank has an account with the central bank and the ability to obtain loans from it.

22 Regarding international relations, including international loans granted to individual countries, the International Monetary Fund plays a significant role. This institution can grant loans in the world's major currencies, but it also issues so-called Special Drawing Rights, which represent a special form of money. Importantly, SDRs are fully convertible into the world's major currencies and can, therefore, be used by lending countries

the economy. First, it is essential to differentiate between the motives for lending by the central bank and those by commercial banks. Central banks are not commercial institutions in the conventional sense, as their main purpose is not to maximize profit. Besides their issuance activities, it can be assumed that central banks perform the following functions in the economy: they are the banks of banks, meaning they maintain the accounts of commercial banks, process interbank payments, and provide them with loans; they serve the public sector by offering banking services to the government; they are responsible for holding and managing currency reserves; they are also guardians of financial system stability, especially the banking system. The central bank that fulfills these tasks also executes monetary policy. This means that the criterion for providing central bank loans and the interest rate on these loans is not profit but rather the fulfillment of the central bank's duties and, in particular, the achievement of monetary policy goals. The goal of central bank monetary policy can be price stability (stability of the value of money) or economic stability, which includes supporting sustainable economic growth (GDP growth) or promoting full employment. Central banks attempt to achieve these goals through a range of monetary policy instruments with which they aim to influence or control exchange rates, the money supply in the economy, or interest rates in the economy.[23]

2.1.4. Effectiveness of Monetary Policy

The effectiveness of central bank policy depends not only on its actions but also on the response of commercial banks and the entire economy. In summary, there are two extremes in understanding the economy and, consequently, the effectiveness of monetary policy. In classical economics, it is assumed that the economy is characterized by flexible prices and wages.[24] In contrast, the Keynesian school argues that prices and wages are not flexible. Adopting either position or an intermediate one has fundamental consequences for understanding the role of monetary policy in the economy. According to the classical view, money has no

---

according to their needs. For more information, see, e.g., The International Monetary Fund (2023b).

23 An overview of the monetary policy frameworks adopted by different countries worldwide is published annually by the International Monetary Fund. See The International Monetary Fund (2023a).

24 In the simplest sense, this involves so-called price elasticity, i.e., the strength of the price response to changes in the economy, such as changes in demand for a particular good. For more on elasticity, see, e.g., Taylor & Weerapana, (2010, pp. 634–635, 736–738).

significance for the real economy, meaning it has no impact on employment levels, real production, real prices, and real interest rates. In other words, it is neutral for the economy, merely acting as a monetary veil that, to a certain extent, only obscures the real economy.[25] From this perspective, it follows that monetary policy is irrelevant to the real economy.[26]

Advocates of opposing views argue that monetary policy can influence real variables in the economy. Currently, those responsible for monetary policy take a middle ground. For example, the European Central Bank formulates its approach as follows: "The neutrality of money is a widely accepted and empirically validated proposition in the economic profession. In the long run, that is, after all adjustments in the economy have worked through, a change in the quantity of money in the economy (all other things being equal) will be reflected in a change in the general level of prices and will not induce permanent changes in real variables such as real output or employment. A change in the quantity of money in circulation ultimately represents a change in the unit of account (and thereby the general price level) which leaves all other variables unchanged."[27]

So, what can monetary policy do today? The central bank, as the issuer of money needed by commercial banks to create money for the economy, can control the money supply and the price of money provision, that is, the central bank's interest rate. This, in turn, can be translated into the value of money in the economy through the so-called transmission mechanism of monetary policy impulses to the economy.[28] Even though, as the classical economists would prefer, inflation is exclusively a monetary phenomenon, price stability is a value. It contributes to a greater potential for economic growth. In summary, by aiming for price stability and keeping an eye on the stability of the banking system as the primary supplier of money to the economy, the central bank contributes to creating conditions conducive to economic development.

---

25 For more about the neutrality of money, see, e.g., Walsh (2003, pp. 200–211).

26 One consequence of such an assumption was the creation of economic models that did not take money into account, effectively assuming a barter economy. See Smithin (2006, p. 1).

27 European Central Bank (2011, p. 55). What determines long-term real economic development are factors such as technological development, demographics, individual preferences of economic agents, and the institutional framework of the economy, including regulations affecting economic and social life, as well as government fiscal policy.

28 A very detailed description of the transmission mechanism can be found, e.g., in Bofinger et al. (2001, pp. 71–124).

2.1.5. Lending by Commercial Banks

Commercial banks, as the name suggests, are institutions whose purpose is to generate profit.[29] One of the most important, and in many cases, the primary source of income for them is the revenue they receive from lending. Credit is a specific product because, firstly, it binds the borrower and the lender together for the entire contract duration, which can last several years. Secondly, granting credit to a customer always involves risk. This is because the customer will repay the credit in the future, which is not predictable in advance. The fact that a customer has creditworthiness today does not mean they will have it in one or ten years (for example, whether they will still be healthy or have sufficient income), and this is influenced by factors dependent on the borrower but also factors independent of them (for instance, job loss not due to laziness but, for example, due to a viral epidemic).[30] Therefore, the main task of the bank in lending is to assess the individual creditworthiness of the customer and structure the pool of all credits (e.g., through various customer diversifications) in a way that reduces the risk to an acceptable level.[31] This means that banks, in carrying out their credit policies, are guided not only by the customer's creditworthiness but also by their own financial situation and the overall economic conditions. Hence, not every needy individual can obtain a loan, and not everyone who receives a loan will bear the same costs for servicing it. In many cases, banks also pass on a portion of the risks to the borrower, especially regarding interest rate and exchange rate risk. A customer taking a foreign currency loan or a variable interest rate loan must consider the fact that the price of currencies or interest rates can change in the future.

In summary, the purpose of banking activity is not to maximize the supply of credit but to maximize profit. To achieve this, banks ration credit (i.e., they do

29 The core business activities of commercial banks include maintenance of current and savings accounts, including time deposits, provision of credit and loans, settlement of payment transactions, and others (e.g., foreign exchange transactions, securities transactions).

30 This also means that banks are more inclined to grant loans to wealthy individuals, people with good jobs, assets, or prosperous businesses. Conversely, poor people without income, occupation, or assets are treated by banks as higher risk subjects.

31 There are primarily three types of risks: credit risk, interest rate risk, and liquidity risk. It is impossible to eliminate risk from banking, so it can be said that risk management is the primary task of banks. Accessible descriptions of bank risks can be found, among others, in Gischer et al. (2020, pp. 119–126).

not grant loans to everyone willing), monitor loan repayment to prevent arrears, and if the borrower becomes insolvent, they attempt to enforce their claims. They do this, firstly, in their own interest and, secondly, in the interest of all customers who hold accounts with the bank and thereby retain their money.[32]

2.2. Sociology of Money

Sociological theories have often adopted an understanding of money as found in economics, either viewing it as a commodity or as credit. Based on such fundamental notions, sociological studies have been conducted, seeking to answer two fundamental questions: How does money function in society, and how does a society using money operate?

The classic authors who explored money around the turn of the 19th to the 20th century were Karl Marx and Georg Simmel.[33] The former regarded money as the universal form of commodities, while the latter saw it as a claim on society. From the 1930s to the 1980s, sociological theories of money saw little development. It was only since the financial crises of the 1990s, particularly the global financial crisis of 2007/2008, that interest in money as a subject of sociological analysis has significantly increased, marking a renaissance of the sociology of money.[34] Recent authors have described money as various things, such as diffuse social media (Zelizer), a social technology (Ingham; Smithin), an instrument of collective memory (Hart), a social process of commensuration (Maurer), or a communal illusion (Karatani).[35]

Many sociological analyses start from the instrumental use of money. Beginning with the understanding of money as a commodity, economics defines it through its functions in exchange.[36] Sociology also examines the functions of

32 The scheme of the nature of banking activity presented here does not rule out a lack of professionalism on the part of banks, malicious intent, or even unethical behavior in individual situations. However, these are not the rule and cannot be the rule, as they would lead to the bankruptcy of such an institution.

33 Cf. Marx (1989); Simmel (2009).

34 Cf. Brugger & Tackner (2020, pp. 23–24); Paul (2012, p. 68).

35 Cf. Dodd (2016, p. 8). Commensuration can be defined as a sociological process by which qualitative differences are reduced to quantitative differences, "by returning to counting and measuring, and by measuring and comparing things or facts using a common unit of measurement." Distelhorst et al. (2014, p. 80). For more on this, see Espeland & Stevens (1998).

36 Cf. Paul (2012, p. 64).

money but highlights its broader significance beyond purely economic perspectives. Money, as a medium of exchange, contributes to effective specialization and the exchange of goods, thus fostering the development of a nation's wealth. As a store of value, by preserving value longer than required in barter, money creates space for freedom and flexibility in the world. Finally, money, as a unit of account, facilitates or even enables the calculation of prices and potential costs and benefits, serving as a tool for rationalizing societal life.[37]

Since many sociologists viewed money as a mere medium of exchange, it is worth starting with an example of such an approach, specifically that of Karl Marx, a classic figure in sociological thought.

2.2.1. Karl Marx

Marx's written contributions on the subject of money are substantial, with money being a recurring theme in several of his works. However, the focus of this analysis will be on what Marx wrote about money in the second and third chapters of the first section of the first volume of "Capital."[38] The approach presented in this work seems to fully reflect Marx's position regarding money as a medium of exchange.

To understand Karl Marx's perspective on money, one must consider that he analyzed the economy of commodity production. In commodity production, the products of human labor take the form of commodities.[39] For Marx, a commodity is "an external object, a thing that satisfies human needs of some kind through its properties."[40] Commodities are, therefore, useful to people, meaning they have a use-value. In addition to use-value, commodities also possess an exchange value, which Marx simply refers to as "value."[41] Exchange value allows for the comparison of different commodities and ultimately their exchange. But what is the common basis for determining the value of a commodity? For Marx, exchange value is "objectified human labor," and the magnitude of value is determined by "the quantity of socially necessary labor time required for their production."[42]

---

37 Cf. Ingham (2004, pp. 3–4).

38 Cf. Marx (1989).

39 For Marx, "all commodities (...) are values objectified human labor" (1989, p. 119).

40 „ein äußerer Gegenstand, ein Ding, das durch seine Eigenschaften menschliche Bedürfnisse irgend einer Art befriedigt" (Marx, 1989, p. 63).

41 For Marx, a commodity does not just have value; it is value in itself. See Marx (1989, p. 81).

42 Marx (1989, p. 71).

How does money emerge in the economy? Marx views money as a commodity that spontaneously arises as a necessary element of the circulation process.[43] Owners of commodities can indirectly compare the value of their commodities with the value of all other commodities on the market because certain commodities function as a general equivalent. The value of each commodity is directly compared with the value of the general equivalent, indirectly relating the values of all other goods to one another. Money is a general equivalent for any commodity (Marx calls it the "universal commodity") because all other commodities are only specific equivalents of money (referred to as "specific commodities").[44]

The uniqueness of money lies in it being a commodity whose use-value doubles within the social process. Money, just like other commodities, has a normal use-value. However, money also has a formal use-value. The formal use-value should not be understood as if the exchange process of a commodity imparts an (additional) value, but rather as a distinct form of value.[45] This new form, known as the money form, can be defined as a value form of the commodity that is independent of its own use-value or the individual needs of the exchange participants.[46] Marx illustrates that, for him, the money form is "only the reflection of the relationships between all other commodities" adhering to a particular commodity.[47] The money form "attaches itself" to the commodity that has become an equivalent in exchange.

---

43 Lapatsioras and Milios suggest that there is a significant conceptual difference in how the concept of money is constructed between "Capital" and "Grundrisse" and in the way the structure of the arguments is constructed in these two works. In "Grundrisse," money is understood as a "symbol." On the one hand, the commodity has a double existence, and this must be reproduced through the process of "symbolization." On the other hand, in the xA = yB exchange relationship, there is a notional third that should be hypostatized in material form. See Lapatsioras & Milios (2012, p. 521).

44 Elsewhere, Marx calls money "commodity absolutely alienable" because it is "the alienated form of all other commodities or the product of their universal alienation," i.e., with money, one can buy any commodity, and any commodity can be sold for money. See Marx (1989, p. 132).

45 Here Marx contradicts some of the views that regard money as more or less than just a commodity. For him, money is, on the one hand, a commodity and, on the other, not just a mere token. Moreover, what can be called a monetary value is not some new imaginary value, but only a form of value.

46 Cf. Marx (1989, p. 115).

47 "nur der an einer Waare festhaftende Reflex der Beziehungen aller andern Waaren" (Marx, 1989, p. 116).

According to Marx, the formal use-value of money arises from its specific social functions. Marx characterizes money with regard to four functions: money as a measure of value in price determination, money as a medium of circulation for the immediate payment of goods, money as a means of payment for settling obligations from past deliveries, and money as a means of accumulating wealth when not in circulation.

In theory, any commodity can be money, but in practice, as mentioned above, these functions are often performed by precious metals. The reason for this lies, firstly, in the fact that their extraction and monetary form require human labor. Secondly, they are characterized by relatively simple divisibility and recombination. In particular, gold and silver possess natural properties that make them suitable as money. Marx even goes so far as to state that "money by nature is gold and silver."[48]

Money is a commodity and, as such, can assume various external forms. It appears that Marx distinguishes between two actual forms of money: the primary form, which is the bullion form of precious metals (pieces of gold), and secondary forms, such as coins, token coins, and representative tokens.[49] A gold coin is money in which the value of gold corresponds to its nominal value.

There are two reasons why secondary forms of money are created. Firstly, money in the form of gold coins wears down during circulation. Secondly, Marx acknowledges the significance of state power in this context.[50] While a token coin may also take the form of a coin, its real value is less than its nominal value. This category also includes state-issued paper money, for example. This form of money is state-regulated and has a fixed exchange rate. In other words, money moves relatively quickly from hand to hand during commodity exchange. When considering the entire money circulation, this leads, in Marx's metaphorical language, to its functional existence essentially absorbing its material existence. In other words, the function of a medium of exchange becomes independent. Money starts to function as a symbol and can be replaced by other symbols.[51] For Marx, paper money, as a means of circulation, is a gold symbol or a money symbol, symbolically representing what gold ideally represents, namely, the

48 Marx (1989, p. 116).

49 Cf. Marx (1989, p. 146).

50 Just as the establishment of the system of monetary units of measure is the prerogative of the state, it is also one of the privileges of the state to determine and mint the external expression of these units.

51 Cf. Marx (1989, p. 146).

quantitative manifestation of the exchange value of individual commodities, or their price. Paper money can also represent value, meaning it can be a symbol of value, but only insofar as it represents a specific quantity of gold.

It should be noted that Marx also uses the term "Kreditgeld" (credit money).[52] Marx understands this as debt obligations for sold goods appearing on the market and becoming part of circulation. Furthermore, with the development of credit relations, other forms of money characteristic to these relationships emerge, which replace money in the form of gold coins in some areas of circulation.[53] However, Marx does not specify whether credit money refers only to a representative of commodity money or represents an entirely different form of money in essence.

What does the analysis of money reveal about society in Karl Marx's eyes? Money and its creation are not just part of the economic sphere; they are also social phenomena. Monetary relationships obscure the underlying social relationships of production. This means that money acts as a double "veil": first, for the economic forces that control production processes, and second, for the even more fundamental social relationships that form during the production process, that is, the capitalist relations that Marx strongly criticizes.[54] In this context, Marx speaks of the so-called commodity fetish and the money fetish. For Marx, fetishism is "the cult of a submission to the spell of a thing, an object of desire that has power over desire."[55] This submission to commodities leads to a distortion of consciousness and alienation of human beings. Just as there is commodity fetishism, there is also money fetishism. Due to its role as the universal equivalent, money as a fetish plays a particular role in society, as it becomes the basis of economic and political power.[56]

---

52 Cf. Marx (1989, p. 147, 157, 158).

53 Cf. Marx (1989, p. 158). It seems that Marx has treated the topic of credit money here too superficially and vaguely, assuming only that it is an expression of the relationship between the creditor and the debtor. For a proper understanding of money, this is not sufficient because it is not known to what extent such a payment instrument is actually generally accepted in payment for goods or in fulfilling obligations. In this context, the issuer of such an instrument, whether it is a bank or another company, plays a crucial role.

54 Cf. Ingham (2004, pp. 61–62).

55 "der Kult einer Unterwerfung unter den Zauber eines Dings, einem Objekt der Begierde, das Macht über das Begehren hat" (Pfreundschuh, 2020).

56 Cf. Drabińska (2020).

Money also implies power on an individual level. In the context of analyzing money as a means of accumulating wealth, Marx links money to power and greed. He claims that the ability to store commodities in the form of money and the fact that money is a storable commodity arouse greed in people. The desire for wealth is inherently limitless, and with the development of trade, this greed intensifies. Having more money enables individuals to buy newer and more goods continually.[57] Therefore, money is associated with power, which is concentrated in the hands of money owners. It is thus a private power held by private individuals (capitalists). However, despite being a private power, it is socially recognized because money itself is socially recognized. As emphasized by Paul, the sociology of money differs from the economics of money not so much in the subject of their research but rather in how they approach it. Economics builds models assuming that subjects abstract from non-economic circumstances, while sociology is interested in social action as a social relationship. For this reason, sociology finds it insufficient to understand money merely as a means to achieve economic goals. To sociology, money is not just a mediator in various interactions but something that constitutes a specific, highly flexible, and thus effective social relationship.[58] In this context, one can present Georg Simmel's understanding of money.

2.2.2. Georg Simmel

In his book "The Philosophy of Money," Georg Simmel pursues two objectives. Firstly, he wants to address the question: How does money come to have value at all, or in other words: What is the essence of money? Secondly, does the existence of money influence the lives of individuals and societies, and more precisely, does it change them?[59] Simmel justifies his approach to the subject of money by emphasizing that the difference between various sciences can pertain not only to their subject matter but also to their specific methods of approaching the same subject. This is because the results of individual sciences never exhaust the entirety of reality. For example, the exchange of products between two individuals can be examined from economic, psychological, moral, and aesthetic perspectives.[60]

57 "With the expansion of commodity circulation, the power of money, the ever-ready, absolutely social form of wealth, grows" (Marx, 1989, p. 151).

58 Cf. Paul (2012, p. 51).

59 Cf. Simmel (2005, p. 52).

60 Cf. Simmel (2005, p. 53).

In contrast to Marx and other proponents of understanding money as a commodity whose value arises from its specific substance or the properties of the material from which it is made, Simmel posits that money represents an abstract value. Simmel introduces two dimensions of money analysis: (1) money as abstract value and (2) money as a form of socialization, that is, as a construct of social relationships.[61]

For Simmel, (economic) value, is an exchange relationship of goods, and to have economic value means to be exchangeable for something else. With this understanding of value, money is an expression of value, moreover, it is "that which is valuable."[62] However, it is an expression that is independent of goods because money has managed to abstract itself from them. He expresses it as follows: "If the economic value of objects is constituted by their mutual relationship of exchangeability, then money is the autonomous expression of this relationship. Money is the representative of abstract value. From the economic relationship, i.e. the exchangeability of objects, the fact of this relationship is extracted and acquires, in contrast to those objects, a conceptual existence bound to a visible symbol."[63]

This autonomy of money is manifested in its absolute lack of individuality. This means that money, as a relation between things, remains the same, even as the things being exchanged change.[64]

With his emphasis on the abstract nature of money, Georg Simmel highlights its function as a unit of account. This is also evident in his analysis of the development of forms of money. Simmel points out that it seems logical for this development to progress from substance to pure function (pure token money).[65]

For Simmel, money is also a social institution.[66] Its essence and effectiveness, that is, its character as a tool, lie in social organization and supra-subjective norms rather than in its external, material form. The abstract form of money in relation to things arises from the fact that money, in its purest forms, is "the

61 Cf. Ingham (2004, p. 63).
62 Simmel (2005, p. 119).
63 Simmel (2005, p. 118). Elsewhere, Simel defines money as "the reification of the pure relationship between things as expressed in their economic motion" (2005, p. 175).
64 Cf. Simmel (2005, p. 122).
65 Simmel is skeptical, however, about whether this ideal of dematerialized money or pure symbol can be achieved at all. Simmel points to technical limitations as the reason why this goal may not be attainable. Cf. Simmel (2005, p. 163).
66 In this context, Frisby pictures money as a spider that weaves a social web (1984, p. 51).

means" or "the absolute means" or "the means *par excellence*," that is, "[w]hat money mediates is not the possession of an object but the exchange of objects."[67]

More precisely, for Simmel, the essence of money is that it is credit, that is, the representative of a credit relationship.[68] This holds true for every form of money. The essence is the same. Every form of money is merely an instruction to society that its holder (typically) has provided some form of service for which the money was received and is entitled to a refund. Simmel compares money to a bill of exchange with no indication of a specific debtor for the bill. In this case, who is the debtor? Anyone belonging to a particular economic cycle. Simmel expresses it as follows: "The common relationship that the owner of money and the seller have to a social group—the claim of the former to a service and the trust of the latter that this claim will be honoured—provides the sociological constellation in which money transactions, as distinct from barter, are accomplished."[69]

On a sociological level, therefore, there is a connection between money and trust. However, as Simmel observes, the historical development of money was not solely based on trust but on the compulsion of the ruling authorities: "One might say that money becomes increasingly a public institution in the strict sense of the word; it consists more and more of what public authorities, public institutions and the various forms of intercourse and guarantees of the general public make of money, and the extent to which they legitimize it."[70]

This is Simmel's core understanding of money. Money, originally rooted in the private realm, becomes a social institution with the social and economic development of humanity. Moreover, as civilization advances, the significance of money increases. It becomes an element that permeates nearly all human interactions. It creates a kind of relationship based on the flow of goods and services.[71] This, in turn, contributes to peaceful coexistence among people because, through exchange, they "accept a supra-personal and normative regulation."[72] In other words, money establishes a common basis of understanding for people that is acceptable to both sides of the exchange. Consequently, money is also a carrier of individual freedom. Through money, the final separation between a person as an individual and a person as an instrument has been achieved. The

67 Simmel (2005, p. 211).
68 Cf. Simmel (2005, pp. 177–178).
69 Simmel (2005, p. 177).
70 Simmel (2005, p. 183).
71 Cf. Deflem (2003, p. 70).
72 Simmel (2005, p. 95).

gift of freedom that money gives to humans enables them to shape their lives freely, even in the economic realm. Simmel illustrates this with an example of how the feudal relationship between landlords and peasants changed after the introduction of money: “The lord of the manor who can demand a quantity of beer or poultry or honey from a serf thereby determines the activity of the latter in a certain direction. But the moment he imposes merely a money levy the peasant is free, in so far as he can decide whether to keep bees or cattle or anything else.”[73] But not only that, money also offers a form of protection from culture. Simmel puts it this way: “The pecuniary character of relationships, either openly or concealed in a thousand forms, places an invisible functional distance between people that is an inner protection and neutralization against the overcrowded proximity and friction of our cultural life.”[74]

On the other hand, money can become an end in itself. This is because, in its case, the quantity of money is perceived as its quality, that is, the perception of its quality increases with the quantity of money. Simmel formulates it as follows: “[O]ne of the major tendencies of life—the reduction of quality to quantity—achieves its highest and uniquely perfect representation in money. Here too, money is the pinnacle of a cultural historical series of developments which unambiguously determines its direction.”[75] In this case, one can speak of the commodification of almost every level of social relationships. This can manifest in various ways, such as greed, miserliness, passion for acquisition, wastefulness, or in treating interpersonal relationships through the prism of economic exchange, leading to modern cynicism or world-weariness, among other things.[76]

The thesis of money as a social relationship is widely accepted in sociology today. It is defined, for example, as follows: “Money is a social relation of credit and debt denominated in a money of account.”[77] Money as such a relationship can be understood in three senses: (1) It is produced outside the market, that is, it is neither produced by market participants nor subject to market laws regarding other goods. The creation of money as a means of payment or unit of account is the domain of legally sanctioned entities (states, banks), and its provision is

73 Simmel (2005, p. 286).
74 Simmel (2005, p. 483).
75 Simmel (2005, p. 281)..
76 Cf. Simmel (2005, pp. 260–282).
77 Ingham (2004, p. 12). In a similar vein, the nature of money is formulated by Paul, for whom money is at its “core a form of credit” (Paul, 2012, p. 64).

not subject to market regulations. (2) Exchange with money significantly differs from barter because it creates a new social relationship, a relationship not between two but three persons, namely the buyer, the seller, and the issuer of money.[78] (3) Contemporary capitalist money is merely a symbol of the payment promises of its guarantors and issuers, that is, states and banks.[79] The holder of money is in a creditor-debtor relationship with the issuer of the money. For such a relationship to be accepted by the creditor, the debt repayment must be enforceable, requiring the existence of an appropriate authority. Hence Ingham's thesis that money is a form of sovereignty.[80]

2.2.3. Talcott Parsons

An interesting aspect of sociological research on money is its symbolic nature. Money is a symbolic medium, that is, a symbolic, generalized means of communication and interaction. Its function boils down to the integration of functionally different parts of the social system.[81] For example, Parsons illustrates the function of a symbol in society in this way: "Especially where there is social interaction, signs and symbols acquire common meanings and serve as media of communication between actors. When symbolic systems which can mediate communication have emerged we may speak of the beginning of a 'culture' which becomes part of the action systems of the relevant actors."[82] Symbols, therefore, play a culture-creating role in society. For Parsons, money is one of these symbols that function within the social reward system. It is proof of success and a means of exercising power.[83]

Sociologists agree that money shapes society. Ingham describes money as one of the most crucial social technologies to which humanity owes its

78 Paul describes it as follows: "Money is the third (der Dritte)—precisely, it should be said, a third (ein Dritter), because there are others—that joins the actors involved in exchange and transforms it into an event, a form or a system of its own right. It is not an intermediary whose service could in principle be dispensed with, but the expression and center of a *menage a trois*" (Paul, 2012, p. 64).

79 Cf. Ingham (2006, pp. 22–23).

80 This does not mean that the state must be the sole issuer of money, but rather that the state must protect the creditor's right to enforce its debts.

81 Cf. Ingham (2004, p. 60).

82 Parsons (1951, p. 5).

83 Cf. Parsons (1951, p. 247).

development.[84] One of the classics, alongside Marx and Simmel, who examined the social impacts of money, was Max Weber.

2.2.4. Max Weber

The topic of money appears in Max Weber's work in the context of his considerations on the process of rationalization in industrial society.[85] In this process, the Protestant ethic played a significant role in shaping the development of capitalist and modern society.[86]

Weber observes that the emergence of money in the economy and, in a broader sense, in society changed and increased economic opportunities by (1) contributing to the development of trade by enabling what is known as "indirect exchange," (2) enabling value to be stored in money and thus ensuring the possibility of acquiring goods and services in the future, (3) enabling liabilities to be measured in monetary terms.

As a result, the aim of human activity was to have more money available and to calculate expenditures in such a way that they could be covered by the foreseeable income.[87]

All these social changes were possible because the most crucial feature of money (which Weber refers to as the "most important fact of all") is its function as a unit of account that enables monetary calculation. According to Weber, using money as the unit of account is the possibility of estimating in money all the goods and services that can be considered for exchange.[88] The introduction of money as a unit of account, or the development of accounting as it is known

84 Cf. Ingham (2004, p. 3). Ingham does not define the term "social technology," but he seems to understand it as a product or invention of a human being that influences social processes. Ingham does not address the question of whether money is a conscious and planned product of the application of sociological knowledge or a natural and spontaneous creation within human relationships. Today's understanding of social technology is somewhat different, as it implies the deliberate use of sociological knowledge to influence society. Cf. Knoblauch (2006).

85 Weber's concept of rationalization (*Rationalisierung*) is an ambiguous term. In the context quoted here, it means an attitude dominated by success, efficiency, technical rationality, or functionality in today's world. Despite its destructive potential, such a form of rationality is a prerequisite for material and cultural wealth today. Cf. Hellmich (2013, p. 18).

86 Cf. Deflem (2003, pp. 76–77).

87 Cf. Weber (1978, pp. 80–81).

88 Cf. Weber (1978, p. 81).

today, enabled monetary calculation and rationalized not only the private sphere but also public bureaucracy.[89]

Finally, it should be mentioned that for Weber money is not and cannot be neutral. It "can never be merely a harmless 'voucher' or a purely nominal unit of accounting so long as it is money."[90] Its value depends on its availability, which in turn is the result of the clash of various interests. The value of money thus results from these interests.

What applies to money also holds true for the prices of all goods and services offered on the market. Weber expresses it as follows: "In a market economy every form of rational calculation, especially of capital accounting, is oriented to expectations of prices and their changes as they are determined by the conflicts of interests in bargaining and competition and the resolution of these conflicts. (…) Capital accounting in its formally most rational shape thus presupposes the battle of man with man."[91]

For Weber, this is also an argument against the possibility of conducting rational monetary calculations in a socialist economy. This is because bureaucracy is unable to create money that would be the result of reconciling various interest groups. Bureaucracy typically represents the interests of the state and not necessarily the interests of all groups in society and the economy.

The brief description of the sociology of money presented here illustrates how a sociological approach can significantly enrich the economic understanding of money.

2.3. Psychology of Money

The psychology of money begins with the simple observation that money is a ubiquitous presence in human life. People not only earn or spend money, but they also talk about it and sometimes even argue over it. Money can also serve as inspiration for artists, for example.

In psychology, money itself is considered inert, but when it acquires special significance, it gains extraordinary power. Therefore, psychology is interested in understanding people's attitudes toward money. Psychology examines why and how people behave with and toward money and what impact it has on human relationships.[92]

---

89 Weber is close to Knapp's understanding of money. See Ingham (2004, pp. 66–67).
90 Weber (1978, p. 79).
91 Weber (1978, pp. 92–93).
92 Cf. Furnham (2014, p. 2).

The psychological approach to money seeks to answer the question of how money influences human actions, particularly addressing the question: "How does money affect the minds, brains, and behavior of people?" It investigates reactions to money on both psychological and biological levels, which influence human behavior.[93]

From a psychological perspective, money is seen as a biological incentive that stimulates or directs human behavior or as a cultural invention that influences people's thinking and actions within a particular culture due to its significance.

2.3.1. Money as a Biological Incentive

The starting point of the first approach is to compare the biological response of humans to money with the response of animals to food or drink. In nature, living organisms develop reactions and behaviors that allow them to search for and obtain food in an optimal manner (e.g., bees learn to avoid flowers with little nectar and find those with a relatively high amount of such food). The acquisition of food serves as a reward for the development of effective behavior. Psychological research has demonstrated that practically any object can become a reward, meaning that virtually any object can be assigned a reward value.[94]

Money holds great value for humans because it can be used to purchase almost anything that satisfies human needs. In this sense, money can be treated as a substitute for goods and services, and its possession can be considered a reward.[95]

In seeking an answer to how money can satisfy biologically rooted human needs and desires, Lea and Webley proposed two complementary theories of money. First, they view money as a tool in a metaphorical sense, or more precisely, as a means to achieve a goal. The goal is to obtain goods that satisfy the needs of a specific individual. Second, the use of money goes beyond its instrumental function. Money can have a similar effect to a drug that affects the normal functioning of the nervous system.[96]

More specifically, money can influence people in the same way as pharmacological agents that enhance human satisfaction.[97] Money can stimulate the same brain centers responsible for happiness, contentment, joy, and motivation

93 Cf. Bijleveld & Aarts (2015, p. 3).
94 Cf. Bijleveld & Aarts (2015, pp. 4–6).
95 Cf. Bijleveld & Aarts (2015, pp. 4–6).
96 Cf. Lea & Webley (2006, pp. 163–165).
97 Cf. Lea & Webley (2015, p. 23).

(the mesolimbic system). However, this also means that people can become dependent on money. Detailed research in this area pertains to pathological gambling, which is considered a disease. The consequences of such addiction have significant personal and social impacts (depression, divorce, homelessness, suicide).[98]

This approach, supported by neurocognitive research, has inspired analyses that examine how money activates reward centers in the brain and how this response differs from animal reactions. It also explores the factors that shape human perception of money and when and how money has a motivating effect on people.[99] In this context, noteworthy is the detailed research on the effects of money-related stimuli on the human mind and brain. For example, there are studies on which parts of the brain are affected by money, how the human brain responds to such a stimulus both at the level of consciousness and in situations before money becomes consciously recognized.[100] It has been shown, among other things, that money can motivate people and change their behavior even when they are unaware of it.[101] Furthermore, research investigates how and for what reasons people attribute subjective value to a specific amount of money and how the perception of money changes with age.[102]

2.3.2. Money as a Cultural Creation

In the second case mentioned above, money is regarded as a cultural product that was created in early agricultural societies.

The starting point is the observation that with the transition of original human communities from hunter-gatherer societies to agricultural ones, these communities grew in number as they developed more efficient methods for acquiring and storing food. This also increased the exchange of goods and services. These reasons led to the development of rules that ascribed value to certain things and determined the amount of this value. These objects were also used as money in trade.

The objects used as money also had other functions. Anthropological research has shown that such objects were placed alongside the deceased in graves, used in religious ceremonies, and adorned the walls with the first money they

98 Cf. Huberfeld & Dannon (2015, pp. 163–185).
99 Cf. Bijleveld & Aarts (2015, pp. 4–6).
100 Cf. Krug & Braver (2015, pp. 137–162).
101 Cf. Capa & Custers (2015, pp. 73–91).
102 Cf. Buechel et al. (2014, pp. 93–120); Samanez-Larkin et al. (2015, pp. 121–135).

earned.[103] These examples demonstrate that humans, as social beings, assign meaning to their environment. As Bijleveld and Aarts emphasize, interpreting the impulses that humans receive from their surroundings is one of the greatest challenges in social life. Among these stimuli, it is perhaps most difficult to interpret those generated by words, attitudes, and the behavior of other people. Money and money-related activities also belong to the stimuli to which a person attributes meaning (meaning-making process), influencing their perception of reality.[104] For example, receiving payment can motivate people to exert more effort and perform better because when someone is paid for something (e.g., performing an action), their need for competence, the feeling of being useful and proficient in something, can be satisfied. On the other hand, payment can also discourage people from doing something because it may threaten their sense of autonomy (if I receive money for something, I am obligated to do it).[105]

In this context, it is argued that it is easier to attribute additional meanings to modern money (non-exchange-related associations) since modern forms of money practically have no utility value but only an exchangeable value, meaning the value of what they represent (goods and services they can be used to purchase). Furthermore, money can more easily be associated with specific cultural categories (e.g., power), behaviors (e.g., peacocking), or justifications for life decisions (e.g., an independent lifestyle).[106]

Not only earning money but also spending money has psychological implications. This is because spending money is seen as both a situation of gain and loss. Gain is associated with the satisfaction of specific needs through the purchased goods, while loss relates to what is referred to in economics as opportunity costs, meaning that when you have only a limited amount of money, buying one thing automatically means losing the opportunity to buy another. Which of these two experiences and emotions is stronger can be determined by the purchased object (material or immaterial), the social consequences of the purchase (whether it strengthens social bonds or not), and even the form of money used for the purchase (cash or cashless).[107]

The conclusions of the above-mentioned studies align with Fiske's theory that social life is based on four structures of human attitudes. One of these structures,

---

103 Cf. Bijleveld & Aarts (2015, pp. 3–6).
104 Cf. Bijleveld & Aarts (2015, pp. 14–16).
105 Cf. Moller & Deci (2015, pp. 189–211).
106 Cf. Bijleveld & Aarts (2015, pp. 3–6).
107 Cf. Carter (2015, pp. 213–242).

possibly arising with the creation of money, is the so-called market-pricing model. In this model, social relationships are organized through the prism of cost-benefit ratios and rational calculations of efficiency and expected utility. For Fiske, money is the prototypical medium of such a structure.[108] This also means that not only the use of money alone can have certain psychological and social consequences, but even the perception of money (experiments have been conducted where people were shown money, and their reactions were examined) can make people more egocentric and selfish, deteriorating their social relationships. This is primarily manifested in people preferring independence, working independently, helping others less, and forming fewer new acquaintances.[109]

2.4. Ethics of Money

The subject of the ethics of money, as the name suggests, is not money itself, but rather the human and their attitude toward money. As Kramer rightly notes: "It is only the way people handle money that determines whether good or evil is done with it."[110] Money ethics should therefore, on the one hand, deal with the individual, subjective handling of money, especially concerning the use of one's own money and the management of others' money (trust money). Therefore, this ethics should primarily concern income earners, consumers, and savers as its entities. Furthermore, money ethics should develop ethical standards and behavioral rules for financial intermediaries (including financial markets).[111] Ethical considerations related directly or indirectly to money can be divided into three areas: (1) the question of whether financial activities (and money) are always morally suspicious, (2) the question of integrity in financial markets, and

---

108 Cf. Fiske (1992, pp. 691–692, 706–708, 717). The other three forms of human relationships are: communal sharing, authority ranking, and equality matching.

109 Cf. Mead & Stuppy (2015, pp. 243–262); Vohs et al. (2006, pp. 1154–1156, 2008, pp. 208–212).

110 "Erst des Menschen Umgang mit dem Geld bestimmt, ob mit dem Geld Gutes oder Böses geschieht" (Kramer, 1996, p. 18).

111 In addition to ethics of money, currency ethics and financial ethics stand out. The domain of currency ethics is expected to address questions about an orderly monetary system, i.e., the relationship between national and international monetary systems, and especially the problems associated with money creation and the proper conditions for the functioning of money. Financial ethics, on the other hand, is supposed to deal with the ethical dimension of government financial policy, i.e., the issue of just distribution and redistribution of public funds within the economy, including the question of fair taxation. Cf. Schmitz (2004, pp. 196–198).

(3) the question of the social responsibility of financial institutions. Due to the complexity of the topic, only the first area will be presented here, which can strictly be referred to as the ethics of money, namely the question of whether money is the root of all evil.[112]

The history of ethical considerations has been dominated by a negative understanding of money itself and finance.[113] The criticism traditionally encompasses three main areas: (1) the love of money (the profit motive), (2) usury (lending money at excessive interest rates), and (3) speculation (and gambling) in finance.[114]

2.4.1. Love of Money

The love of money can be understood as an action aimed at acquiring money, or more precisely, as a profit-oriented action. When such love becomes absolute, it leads to excessive, irrational economic expansion, is incompatible with the demand for human justice, and even contradicts humanity derived from faith, hope, and love.[115] Criticism of such a motive of human behavior takes three forms:

(a) It is claimed that the profit motive has something unnatural about it. This criticism comes from Aristotle, who presented various forms of trade and wealth acquisition in "Politics." Aristotle distinguished between two arts of acquiring wealth: economics, whose purpose is to acquire goods necessary to satisfy household needs, and chrematistics, the art of accumulating money (or money-making). The first of these arts is in harmony with nature, while the second is against it. Chrematistics is unnatural because the accumulation of money and the multiplication of financial assets become an end in itself. Speculation, that is, trade whose purpose is to increase money, does not satisfy any human needs and, as such, knows no bounds.[116]

(b) The love of money, manifested in the pursuit of wealth, leads to a constant desire for more money. This attitude is usually associated with egoism, greed, and ruthlessness. However, the essence of the economy is cooperation.

112 For more on Questions 2 and 3, see Bruin et al. (2018).

113 The reason for this may have been a simplified and distorted understanding of the words of 1 Timothy 6:10.

114 Cf. Bruin et al. (2018).

115 Cf. Rich (1992, p. 38).

116 Cf. Aristotle (1998, bk. I, 8, 1256b-I, 10, 1258b).

Cooperation means striving for "cooperative productivity."[117] In this context, the profit motive seems to contradict not only economic but also moral principles because it contradicts the principle of cooperation. People who are guided solely by the profit motive are focused only on themselves.[118] This also means that they are capable of ruthless actions, as demonstrated by the behavior of some bankers who would do anything for money.[119]

(c) The love of money as a motive for human action may imply that there are no other, more suitable motives for action. This argument is based on a Kantian understanding of ethics. For Kant, humans are rational beings. It follows that there is a universal human moral law that applies a priori to every individual. This law is known in the conscience of every person as an unconditional duty, an order that motivates them to behave in a certain way.[120] The fundamental question within Kantian ethics is therefore: What should I do?[121] Kant answers this question in the form of so-called the Formula of Humanity. It is worth quoting one of them here: "So act that you use humanity, whether in your own person or in the person of any other, always at the same time as an end, never merely as a means."[122] Therefore, any action that has a purpose other than that of a human being is an instrumental action of that human being, making a person a means, and therefore, from

117 Cf. Reifner (2017, p. 122).

118 An interesting observation is made by Reifner. He believes that greed is a natural driving force for human activity in society. Greed only becomes a problem when it transforms into avarice and stinginess. Cf. Reifner (2017, pp. 122–126).

119 High incomes, especially those of middle and upper-level employees in financial institutions, are associated with ruthlessness and unethical behavior of these individuals, which should have led to the financial crisis of 2008. Cf. Bruin et al. (2018).

120 Cf. Anzenbacher (2001, pp. 50–61).

121 By placing the question of duty at the center of his considerations, Immanuel Kant's approach is called deontological. Alternative approaches are teleological (or purpose-oriented) consequentialism, especially utilitarianism and contractualism. Cf. Düwell et al. (2011, p. 10). In the first case, the moral value of actions is measured by their consequences, especially in the utilitarian approach, i.e., what is useful is good, i.e., what maximizes positive effects for those affected (e.g., Jeremy Bentham, John Stuart Mill), and contractualism (e.g., Thomas Hobbes). In the second approach, morality is what has been recognized as such by a social contract (e.g., Thomas Hobbes).

122 Kant (1998, pt. 4:429). In the German original the formula reads as follows: "Handle so, daß du die Menschheit sowohl in deiner Person, als in der Person eines jeden andern jederzeit zugleich als Zweck, niemals bloß als Mittel brauchst" (Kant, 1902, pt. 429).

> the Kantian perspective, not moral. The love of money seems to exclude the central position of humanity, which is why it is questionable within the framework of Kantian ethics.

However, can the love of money as a motive for human action be defended in any way? To achieve this, one can try to point out that either the pursuit of the profit motive itself is good, or at least an action motivated by it brings about good side effects.

Max Weber finds the first position in Protestant ethics. In his view, Protestant ethics aim both at frugal living and at earning and acquiring money. He expresses it as follows: "In fact, the *summum bonum* of this ethic, the earning of more and more money, combined with the strict avoidance of all spontaneous enjoyment of life, is above all completely devoid of any eudæmonistic, not to say hedonistic, admixture. It is thought of so purely as an end in itself, that from the point of view of the happiness of, or utility to, the single individual, it appears entirely transcendental and absolutely irrational."[123]

The second position is represented by Adam Smith. He formulates the concept of the invisible hand of the market, that is, the mechanism through which self-interested economic activities have positive effects on others. Smith says: "By preferring the support of domestic to that of foreign industry, he intends only his own security; and by directing that industry in such a manner as its produce may be of the greatest value, he intends only his own gain, and he is in this, as in many other cases, led by an invisible hand to promote an end which was no part of his intention. Nor is it always the worse for the society that it was no part of it. By pursuing his own interest he frequently promotes that of the society more effectually than when he really intends to promote it. I have never known much good done by those who affected to trade for the public good. It is an affectation, indeed, not very common among merchants, and very few words need be employed in dissuading them from it."[124]

It is worth mentioning the proposals of Walsh and Lynch, who argue that in practice, there are only isolated cases where someone is guided solely by a profit motive. They propose a more nuanced position, in which they distinguish three motives for human actions: (1) Lucrative Action—guided solely by the profit motive (this position is rejected by them from a moral perspective). (2) Accumulative Action—when the profit motive is of primary but not exclusive importance

123 Weber (2013, p. 18).
124 Smith (1776, vol. II, Bk. IV, Ch. II, p. 35).

and can be restricted by moral values such as sensitivity to the necessities and vulnerabilities of needs satisfaction. (3) Stipendiary Action—when profit is only a byproduct of an activity aimed at other goals, including non-commercial purposes.[125]

2.4.2. Usury

One of the most delicate ethical topics in the history of the Church was the question of interest and usury. Ancient and medieval societies were critical of interest rates.[126] Originally, the terms "interest" and "usury" were identical. However, as the practice of granting interest-bearing loans became more prevalent, a distinction was made between interest and a specific form of interest, namely usury, which, in this context, meant the charging of exorbitant interest rates.

For centuries, the Church also held a negative stance toward interest and usury. This position of the Church is primarily derived from Holy Scripture but also has its roots in ancient philosophical thought.

The Old Testament regulations on interest rates and usury can be found in three texts: Ex 22:24, Lev 25:35–37, and Deut 23:20–21. The first and second texts relate to the prohibition of charging interest from a poor Israelite, while the third text prohibits charging interest from any Israelite. However, the book of Deuteronomy adds that interest can be charged on a loan given to a foreigner.[127] In other Old Testament writings, the topic of interest is also mentioned. In Ps 15:5, the Psalmist praises those who do not charge interest on borrowed money, while in Prov 28:8, the author warns against those who accumulate wealth by lending money at interest, as they will be deprived of their riches.[128] On the other hand, the Prophet Ezekiel characterizes someone who does not charge interest on borrowed money (Ezek 18:8, 13, 17) as a just person. He also mentions the cultivation of usury and the collection of interest as sins when reminding of Jerusalem's sins (Ezek 22:12).

---

125 Cf. Walsh & Lynch (2008, pp. 90, 131, 207).

126 For more on interest and usury in the Ancient Near East and Antiquity, see, e.g., Lütge & Uhl (2017, pp. 47–49).

127 A foreigner is meant here as a non-Israelite who has the right of permanent residence among the Israelites (resident alien). Cf. Kaiser et al. (1996, p. 123).

128 Issing is of the opinion that equating money with wealth or assets is a linguistic negligence. Consequently, all allegations of wealth acquisition and distribution are traced back to money. See Issing (1993, col. 331).

In the New Testament, the question of interest and usury is only indirectly addressed. In Jesus' teachings, one can find the acceptance of banking activities and earning interest on a bank account (Parable of the Talents in Mt 25:14–30, especially verse 27, and Lk 19:11–27, especially verse 23). On the other hand, Luke 6:34–35 can be interpreted either as an encouragement for general and unintentional kindness or as a prohibition of granting interest-bearing loans.[129]

The criticism of and often the rejection of interest by the Church also has non-biblical sources. The critical arguments seem to have been twofold: Firstly, it was claimed, following Aristotle, that borrowing at interest is not compatible with nature. Lending money at interest, as an area of chrematistics, was classified by Aristotle as a type of money-making that goes against nature. He wrote: "The trade of the petty usurer is hated with most reason: it makes a profit from currency itself, instead of making it from the process which currency was meant to serve. Currency came into existence merely as a means of exchange; usury tries to make it increase. This is the reason why it got its name; for as the offspring resembles its parent, so the interest bred by money is like the principal which breeds it, and it may be called 'currency the son of currency.' Hence we can understand why, of all modes of acquisition, usury is the most unnatural."[130]

The second critical trend was based on principles of justice and criticism of inequality. The origins of this argument can be traced back to Plato. According to him, loans with interest compound social inequality through their interest effect. He expressed it as follows: "But their targets, stooped businessmen that they are, appear not to notice. They continue to inject the venom of money into any remaining member of the community who submits to them; they continue to collect compound rates of interest, the offspring of the loan, and they continue to fill the community with drones and beggars."[131]

The Church's stance on interest and usury has evolved historically. Already at the Council of Nicaea in 325, the Council Fathers, citing Sacred Scripture, rejected the possibility for the clergy to engage in interest loans: "Since many enrolled [among the clergy] have been induced by greed and avarice to forget the sacred text, 'who does not put out his money at interest' (Ps 15:5—P.K.), and to charge one per cent [a month] on loans, this holy and great synod judges that if any are found after this decision to receive interest by contract or to transact the business in any other way or to charge [a flat rate of] fifty per cent or in general

129 Cf. Kramer (1996, pp. 46–49); Vermeersch (1912).
130 Cf. Aristotle (1998, bk. I, 10, 1258b).
131 Plato (1998, p. 555e).

to devise any other contrivance for the sake of dishonourable gain, they shall be deposed from the clergy and their names struck from the roll."[132] Over a hundred years later, Pope Leo I the Great extended (albeit implicitly) the prohibition of usury to laypeople as well.[133] However, among the Church Fathers, there was no uniform position on the percentage of interest charges. For example, Ambrose of Milan accepted the Old Testament standpoint and believed that interest should not only apply to members of his own faith community. Cyril of Alexandria, on the other hand, believed that interest could not be exacted from anyone. Tertullian held a similar view.[134]

Saint Thomas Aquinas shared and connected the positions of Aristotle and Plato. In his view, charging interest was not permissible due to the nature of money. Money that is involved in exchange is consumed, and interest should not be taken from things that are consumed in their use. Moreover, charging interest for borrowed money means that something non-existent is being sold, which leads to inequality and contradicts justice. As such, it is a sin.[135] However, Saint Thomas acknowledges some external justifications for charging interest. These include the risk of capital loss to the lender (*periculum sortis*) and the damage the lender may have suffered while their money was in the possession of the borrower (*damnum emergens*).[136]

Later thinkers, such as those from the School of Salamanca, continued and further developed Saint Thomas's thinking. In addition to the two external reasons mentioned above, justifying the collection of interest, they added a third. It could be justified to charge interest if the borrower could have made a profit with the borrowed money, even if they did not actually make it (*lucrum cessans*). Other external titles for interest include the so-called *titulus morae*, that is, the contractual penalty, and business contracts (*societates*).[137]

---

132 Canon 17: „Quoniam multi sub regula constituti avaritiam et turpia lucra sectantur, oblitique divinae scripturae, dicentis qui pecuniam suam non dedit ad usuram, cum mutuum dederint, cente-simas exigunt: iuste constituit sancta et magna synodus, ut, si quis inventus fuerit post hanc definitionem usuras accipiens aut per adinventionem aliquam vel quolibet modo negotium transigens authimolia, id est sescupla, exigens vel aliquid tale prorsus excogitans turpis lucri gratia: deiciatur a clero et alienus exsistat a regula" (Baron & Pietras, 2003, p. 43). English translation, Council Fathers (2020).

133 Cf. Saint Leo the Great (1957).

134 Cf. Kramer (1996, pp. 52–53).

135 Cf. Thomas Aquinas (1981, pt. II–II, q. 78, a. 1).

136 Cf. Majka (1986, p. 129).

137 Cf. Majka (1986, pp. 129, 152).

At the beginning of the 16th century, the official position of the Catholic Church on the permissibility of interest also changed slightly.[138] Pope Leo X decided definitively on the question of pawnshops, known as Monti di Pietà (*montes pietatis*), in the bull *Inter multiplices*. The Pope affirmed the interest charged by these banks but with the condition that these interest rates should not exceed the value of the costs incurred by these banks; in other words, they should not be a source of profit.[139]

At the beginning of the 20th century, the Church still held a critical view of usury as a source of profit. The last official document of the Catholic Church that mentioned the topic of usury was the Code of Canon Law of 1917 (Canones 1543 and 2354).[140] There were provisions that prohibited the payment of interest when an object was lent, and that object was returned to its original owner after the loan period expired. By its nature, the loan contract was thus gratuitous.[141] On the other hand, it was permissible to charge moderate (i.e., lawful) interest on loans. Finally, even higher profit could be demanded if it could be considered proportionate and fair. The Code also prescribed penalties for laypeople and clergy convicted of usury. In the later teachings of the Church and in the Code of John Paul II, the topic of usury as such was no longer addressed.[142] However, this does not mean that the Church's stance on usury has fundamentally changed in recent times. During his general audience on February 4, 2004, Pope John Paul II referred to usury as a scourge.[143]

2.4.3. Speculation (and Gambling) in Finance

The issue of speculation (and gambling) in financial markets appears to be the most challenging for ethical analysis. Extreme, populist criticism of financial systems posits that financial markets are casinos and their participants are gamblers.

---

138 Usury, understood as lending at interest, was prohibited at the following councils: Second Lateran Council, Canon 13, Third Lateran Council, Canon 25, Fourth Lateran Council, Constitution 67, Council of Lyon II, Constitution II/26–27, and Council of Vienne, Decree 29. See Baron & Pietras (2005, p. 111, fn. 137).

139 Cf. Fifth Lateran Council (1515), Latin version Leo X. (1901–1927, cols. 905–907).

140 Cf. Catholic Church (1917).

141 Retzbach claims that this canon, although it formally concerned only the situation in which one of the contracting parties was a church person, was in reality binding for all Catholics. See Retzbach (1953, p. 364).

142 Cf. Aymans et al. (2017).

143 Cf. John Paul II (2004b).

Representatives of more balanced opinions attempt to distinguish speculation from other forms of activity in financial markets. However, the problem is that the concept of speculation itself is not clear-cut and is understood differently by many authors.[144] Without delving into detailed conceptual considerations that would require a thorough analysis of how speculative transactions are conducted, the following ethical arguments can generally be made regarding speculation.

Among the critical ethical arguments against speculation and speculators is that they are driven solely by a narrowly defined profit motive, that is, by price changes in financial instruments at their own discretion, rather than by the well-being of the companies that issue them. It is further pointed out that speculation is associated with high risk, and this has not only an individual but also a social dimension (it can, for example, trigger a financial crisis). Finally, the fact that the time horizon of speculative transactions is short affects the actions of speculators and the behavior of other companies in the financial market (e.g., managers of publicly traded companies focus on short-term financial results since they influence the market price of the stocks of the companies they manage).

Defenders of speculation, on the other hand, point to the benefits it brings to financial markets. Speculation facilitates the allocation of funds in the economy, allows non-speculators to protect themselves against risks, and even increases or creates liquidity in financial markets. All these advantages of speculators' actions lead to better functioning financial markets, which is also morally positive.[145]

2.5. Theology of Money

Theology also engages with money. Here, only two drafts of a theology of money will be presented in a rudimentary way.

2.5.1. Nimi Wariboko

One possible proposal for understanding the theology of money can be found in the work of Nimi Wariboko. Such a theology aims to be a theological-ethical reflection on money and monetary phenomena. The starting point for these considerations should be theological thinking, with the goal of creating a financial system that promotes full participation and justice and is oriented toward God's

144 For example, Dembinski introduces both the duration of a deposit (an investment) and the so-called technique of short selling as criteria for distinguishing between saving and speculation. See Dembinski (2017, p. 47).

145 Cf. Bruin et al. (2018).

eschatological future.[146] Wariboko puts it this way: "Theology of money's main task is to provide a theological-ethical framework for understanding money as a social practice and to bring into awareness the ethical principles that can inform efforts to assess and restructure the monetary system, the role of money in human development, and the economic development of countries in the still-open future."[147]

As a basis for his reflections, Wariboko particularly draws on the Trinitarian principles of Paul Tillich and the social Trinitarianism of Miroslav Volf. He uses theological concepts borrowed from these theologians and combines them with the economic ideas of John Maynard Keynes and Robert Guttmann.

For Wariboko, money is, on the one hand, a thing that mediates exchange, but on the other hand, being a medium of exchange is not a permanent attribute of things; rather, it is a social relationship between economic actors. Therefore, he defines it as a relational entity. Money is an inseparable unity between the purely abstract unity of social relationships and the concrete in which it manifests itself. In other words, it is an ongoing process between the object used as money and the social relationship it forms. At the same time, Wariboko points out two dimensions, which he labels as theoretical and theological. First, he asks what money is and notes that it should not be identified with specific forms (whether material or immaterial). Money, as such, is primary; its forms are secondary. The theological aspect manifests itself in the fact that money contains one of the tensions of Trinitarian theology, namely the tension between the concrete and the universal.[148]

He observes that there are many national currencies in the world (which he calls "polimediastic structures"), and there is a tendency for the function of global money to be fulfilled by multiple currencies or a single currency (which he calls "monomediastic structures").[149] To resolve the tension between these two groups of structures, Wariboko proposes a theological model of the global financial system based on the concept of the Trinity and the form of a supranational global currency, which he calls the "Earth Dollar." Such a currency must meet four criteria: First, it must be created and issued by a central, democratically governed institution that Wariboko calls the "earthly central bank."

---

146 Cf. Wariboko (2008, pp. 5–9).

147 Wariboko (2008, p. 222).

148 Cf. Wariboko (2008, pp. 112–116).

149 The core "mediastic" refers to the fact that money is a medium of exchange, i.e., it "resides" between the goods exchanged. See Wariboko (2008, p. 224).

All national central banks would hold their reserves in this global central bank. Second, it must be both an asset and a liability on the balance sheet of both the issuer and the holder. Each country would receive a specific amount of Earth Dollars and could only use up to that amount. When this amount is exhausted, it would have to implement programs in its economy to increase exports and acquire Earth Dollars. Third, it can only be used within a global payment and settlement system, that is, for settlements between countries (national currencies would continue to exist within countries). Fourth, it should be an international extension of all national currencies, meaning that all local currencies should have a fixed exchange rate with the Earth Dollar.

The basis for determining the value of a national currency would be the production and foreign trade of a specific economy and the relative strength of that economy in relation to others. The exchange rates of currencies to the Earth Dollar (and thus the mutual exchange rates of national currencies) should be periodically adjusted based on changes in purchasing power and differences in the trade balances of individual countries. The goal would be to reduce the value of a currency in a country with a trade deficit to make its economy more competitive and increase the value of a currency in a country with a trade surplus to stimulate imports into that country. As a result, this would lead to a leveling of trade balances between countries.[150]

The question arises of how to envision such a Trinitarian financial system. The starting point is the assumption of a non-hierarchical Trinitarian theory. Wariboko understands the Holy Trinity as a community of independent divine persons with symmetrical relationships. In the same way, he considers the relationships that play out in his currency model. Here, the Earth Dollar represents a "communio" of independent national currencies, corresponding to the relationships in the Trinity.[151]

---

150 Cf. Wariboko (2008, pp. 208–222).

151 In this sense, Warioboko writes: "The Earth Dollar is 'communion' of interdependent national currencies and the relations in it are not monarchical, monocentric, or bipolar. (...) All national currencies and their values are related to the Earth Dollar. It is not the mutual perichoresis of national currencies but rather the value conditioning („indwelling") of the Earth Dollar common to all of them that makes the national economies into a 'communion corresponding to the Trinity.'" Wariboko (2008, p. 210). In another place, Wariboko also uses the term "perichoresis" to describe the relationship between national currencies based on the Earth Dollar: "What makes for the perichoresis of the national currencies in the *Earth Dollar* system is not the mutuality of the national currencies; rather it is the indwelling of the *Earth Dollar*

2.5.2. Philip Goodchild

Philip Goodchild presents a different understanding of a theology of money. At the forefront of his considerations is the secularization of the present era. He views it as a reality where the practical conditions of human life are exclusively everyday. Referring to Charles Taylor, Goodchild notes that modern times are characterized by the rejection of all transcendent goals of human life.[152] Humanity has achieved self-liberation. What contemporary individuals strive for is their temporal human flourishing, which is achieved through work, pleasure, and regeneration. What is essential on a human, moral, or social level is no longer anchored in the divine or grace but in human effort and social contract. What was previously represented by religious values has been replaced by the mundane, especially economic values. Additionally, the criterion for reorganizing and structuring today's society has become the ideal of a self-regulating market.[153]

However, this ideal implies that the religious and political spheres of societal life have not only been separated from the economic sphere but have also been subordinated to it. How did this happen? Goodchild identifies three historical forces: (1) industrial growth and associated inventions, including the use of fossil fuels—this enabled humans to influence the world order; (2) deregulation, which contributed to the development of market relationships, including consumption, on a supra-local level; (3) the authority of money, especially the creation of credit money.

Money has become a condition for freedom and prosperity. Without money, I am independent of others; with money, I have the right to claim the products of others' labor. In this sense, others depend on me.[154] Therefore, as Goodchild calls it, money possesses spectral power, which is superior to any human power. Goodchild expresses it vividly: "Attempting to control money is like attempting to seize hold of an image in a mirror or a ghost."[155] The power of money should be sought in how it influences human behavior, analogous to how a religious person engages with prayer, in terms of the time, attention, and devotion

---

common to all of them that makes the various national currencies into some sort of communion that may be like unto the Trinity" (Wariboko, 2008, p. 214).

152 Cf. Taylor (2007).

153 Cf. Polanyi (1978).

154 Cf. Goodchild (2009, pp. xii–xiv).

155 Goodchild (2009, p. 68).

dedicated to it. In today's society, acquiring possessions and increasing wealth has become an obligation, and this is the spiritual power of money.

If religion is understood as something that forms the basis for regulating individual and societal life by serving as a source of authority and sustenance in daily life, then, in the modern world, credit money takes on the role of religion in economic life and, more broadly, in social and political life.[156] However, there is a fundamental difference between economic life and traditionally understood religious life. This difference lies in what Goodchild describes as a lack of awareness. Today, there is no need for religious reflection, that is, there is no need to venerate or even realize the object of religion. A practical approach, that is, earning money, suffices.[157]

Goodchild asserts that since money has only an ideal value, the religion of money has its own theology.[158] Theology deals with ultimate criteria, their sources, and the meaning of human life. The task of theology is to propose lifestyles based on these criteria (values) and to evaluate reality in light of these criteria. The particular calling of theology is to reveal the true nature of wealth. If one accepts the existence of a transcendent being (God), then all these criteria have an eschatological dimension. Conversely, if only the immanent dimension of human life is accepted, then material wealth appears as a source of happiness, benefit, pleasure, prosperity, and even charity. In today's capitalist society, credit money is the instrument through which material prosperity can be achieved. Hence, the appearance of such money, money that serves as a universal measure, means the appearance of money that is the principle of the value of all values.[159]

---

156 Goodchild observes that modern life, even though it has hedonistic moments, is generally ascetic in nature, although it differs from the religious form of asceticism: "If in religious life people renounce enjoyment to achieve spiritual goals, then in modern economic life people renounce their prosperity, labour, and time in the pursuit of money." See Goodchild (2009, p. xv).

157 Cf. Goodchild (2009, p. xv).

158 Cf. Goodchild (2010, p. 228).

159 A similar understanding of modern money is held by Minch. He agrees with Goodchild when he claims that capitalism is essentially a belief system in which money is at the center of all values, as "theos". For Minch, capitalism is also a belief system in which money functions as the highest value or God. This system is a secular continuation of Christian structures, and as such, it falls into false notions of humanity, creation, and the divine. The theoretical basis for such functioning of the system and the "theology of money" at its center is a kind of late modern Gnosticism. The theological and formal structure that the capitalist system imitates is the Incarnation of Christ. The money incarnated in currency becomes the source of temporal salvation

This, in turn, brings about a new order, as all existing values are inevitably reevaluated, and consequently, human beings and reality are reevaluated.[160] Goodchild puts it this way: "Where God promises eternity, money promises the world. Where God offers a delayed reward, money offers a reward in advance. Where God offers himself as grace, money offers itself as a loan. Where God offers spiritual benefits, money offers tangible benefits. Where God accepts all repentant sinners who truly believe, money may be accepted by all who are willing to trust in its value. Where God requires conversion of the soul, money empowers the existing desires and plans of the soul."[161]

So, what is the purpose of a theology of money? Theology of money has the task of understanding the reasons why money is revered today and the living conditions that prevail in such a world. It should show the dedication, sacrifices, and convictions that underlie the modern world. It should demonstrate how individual, social, and political life is shaped by money and, in particular, how human life is perceived through the prism of contracts, accounting, and value determination.[162] Theology of money must first and foremost answer the question of whether the essence of money lies in its opposition to God, justice, or nature (in general, the transcendent); then, whether and how true core values ("the value of values") can manifest in human life. In other words, the theology of money has the task of restoring the reality assumed by money, that is, formulating principles by which economic behavior can be evaluated and alternatives can be proposed.[163]

If money, more specifically credit, is at the heart of the problem, then the transformation of the present world is only possible by creating institutional solutions that emancipate politics and free it from the power of credit. Goodchild postulates the creation of new social institutions that grant credit to those who are worthy of it. By this, he means rejecting the monetary dimension as the sole criterion for granting credit and instead introducing a socially compatible evaluation. Credit should thus be newly subordinated to society and its goals.[164]

---

power for today's people, i.e., its accumulation promises a kind of transcendence of the physical finitude of human beings, i.e., freedom, understood as the right to consume. See Minch (2018).

160 Cf. Goodchild (2009, pp. 4–5).

161 Goodchild (2009, p. 11).

162 Cf. Goodchild (2009, p. xvi).

163 Cf. Goodchild (2009, pp. 6–7).

164 Cf. Goodchild (2009, pp. 24–25).

3. Modern Social Encyclicals as a Framework Regarding the Valuation of Money

3.1. Leo XIII and His Encyclical "Rerum novarum"

The encyclical "Rerum novarum," published by Pope Leo XIII on May 15, 1891, deals with the so-called worker question.[1] Given the conflict between the working class and employers, between the poor and the rich, the aim of the encyclical is to emphasize the need for reconciling and cooperating between these classes. "Each needs the other: capital cannot do without labor, nor labor without capital" (19). The path to this reconciliation includes both population groups becoming aware of their mutual rights and duties. Here, the Pope sees his own task and the task of the Catholic Church's teaching. Because the Church is the "common Mother of rich and poor" (30), it aims to bring these previously opposing groups closer together and foster friendship among them, so that brotherly love can ultimately prevail.[2]

Although the issue of money itself is not explicitly addressed in the encyclical, the Pope formulates a fundamental rule in point 22 that can be the key to interpreting money in the entire later social doctrine of the Church: "(...) it is one thing to have a right to the possession of money and another to have a right to use money as one wills."[3] The Pope distinguishes between money itself and the relationship of humans to money. This is confirmed by the words he writes elsewhere: "As for riches and the other things which men call good and desirable, whether we have them in abundance, or are lacking in them-so far as eternal happiness is concerned—it makes no difference; the only important thing is to use them aright" (21).

---

1 Leo XIII (1891b).

2 Shannon notes that the core of the encyclical is the affirmation and protection of the right to private property because it is a key element in solving many of the world's problems at that time. See Shannon (2005, p. 135).

3 In the original Latin text, the thought reads as follows: "(....) iusta possessio pecuniarum a iusto pecuniarum usu distinguitur". Leo XIII (1891a). The semantic ambiguity of the term "pecunia" allows for different interpretations of the phrase. While the English translation uses the word "money," the German version of the encyclical replaces the word "money" with "possession (Besitz)." Cf. Leo XIII. (2007).

In itself, wealth and therefore money are not inherently evil. Money itself appears to be neutral for the Pope. Moreover, it can be interpreted as a gift from God. It is indeed a natural human right to have both immovable and movable property. If a person (worker) deserves a just reward for their work, they have the right to savings, the right to secure their value, and the right to spend them for any purpose, such as purchasing real estate.[4] The right to purchase and use goods is not only granted to the family but also to the state.

On an individual level, the Pope warns against unchecked greed and sensual pleasure. He also points out that Sunday rest should not be an opportunity for unnecessary expenses or squandering money.

In the realm of interpersonal relationships, the Pope distinguishes between two types of responsibilities: the dictates of justice and the duties of Christian love. According to the former, the rich (employers) must not instrumentalize the workers, meaning they must not view them merely as instruments for profit; they are also obligated to pay a fair wage for labor, and furthermore, they should avoid any abuse of the property of the workers. The worker, on the other hand, must fully and faithfully perform the work agreed upon freely, and must not damage the employer's property or insult the employer. The command of love urges the rich to share their wealth with the needy. Citing St. Thomas Aquinas, the Pope soberly states that the rich have the right first to realize their necessary, fitting, and appropriate expenses. Only after their needs are satisfied is it the duty of the wealthy person to give alms (22).

One of the most important issues addressed in the encyclical is the problem of a just wage. The Pope does not deny that the agreement between the worker and the employer is voluntary. However, he points out that it involves more than just the free will of both parties. This is a demand of natural justice, according to which the salary should provide for the livelihood of the worker, his wife, and his children.[5] The Pope does not specify how much would suffice for a worker. However, he emphasizes that the state should ensure that the worker does not live in poverty but has a secure home, clothing, and food so that he can lead a

---

4 For Leo XIII, a man who engages in gainful employment has the right to a fair wage and the right to freely dispose of that wage. Moreover, the Pope seems to advocate a modest way of life. Someone who can save money can thus increase his private property. The Pope puts forward the following arguments for private property: private property distinguishes us from animals, humans have a right to private property, including a natural right, and the right to property also arises from the duty of the head of the family to support his family. See Shannon (2005, pp. 135–136).

5 Nowhere in this encyclical does the Pope specify what the law of natural justice is.

less difficult and longer life. However, the Pope does not specify which specific instruments the state should use in this regard (34–35).

In summary, Pope Leo XIII seems to have a neutral-positive attitude toward money and wealth. At the same time, he warns against excesses and calls for a Christian approach to money, which means duly considering orientations based not only on the principles of justice but also on the principles of charity.[6]

3.2. Pius XI

In relation to Pope Pius XI, two additional encyclicals will be briefly analyzed alongside the classic social encyclical "Quadragesimo anno."[7]

3.2.1. "Quadragesimo anno"

The fortieth anniversary of the publication of "Rerum novarum" marked the release of Pope Pius XI's encyclical "Quadragesimo Anno."[8] The intention expressed by the Pope in the document, published on May 15, 1931, was to lay the foundations for the creation of a healthy social system. The encyclical consists of an introduction and three parts referring to the past, present, and future. In the first part, the Pope highlights the positive fruits of the encyclical "Rerum novarum." Pius XI calls his predecessor's encyclical the Magna Carta of social order (*Magna socialis ordinis charta*).[9] The second part of the encyclical, containing the Church's social teaching, provides a vision for the future to some extent. It particularly addresses questions of property and the social system. Here, the Pope advocates for a system that could be described as a corporate system.[10]

---

6 The Pope's sober attitude toward money is also reflected in his later encyclicals (although they are not encyclicals that enter into the canon of the Church's social doctrine). In one of his encyclicals, the Pope wishes the Brazilian bishops that the implementation of their plans is not hindered by a lack of money. See Leo XIII. (1899, no. 9), and in another, Leo XIII writes that money is a tool in the hands of enemies of the Church to destroy it. See Leo XIII (1902).

7 Pius XI (1931b).

8 Pius XI (1931b).

9 In the English translation of the encyclical, the wording is as follows: "Magna Charta upon which all Christian activity in the social field ought to be based" (39).

10 Firer Hinze points to two dimensions of the significance of the encyclical "Quadragesimo anno". The encyclical expresses ideas that have had a great influence on Catholic social teaching, i.e. social justice, the common good and subsidiarity. However, what was important for Pope Pius XI, namely the creation of a new socio-economic order

Finally, the third part of the document analyzes the current social and economic situation with a reference to the root cause of the current situation, which is the loss of Christian morals. The Pope calls for renewal by aligning social and economic life with the principles of social justice, the Gospel, and Christian love, to create the material foundation for the development of human personality.[11]

As in the encyclical "Rerum novarum," money itself is not a direct subject of reflection here. However, at some points, Pius XI seems to indirectly refer to money. He does so, for example, when discussing the viability of businesses. The Pope links the level of income from work to the financial situation of the company and emphasizes that it is justified to pay a lower wage than the fair one if the company, due to circumstances not attributable to the entrepreneur, does not have sufficient income to pay a just wage (72).

Pius XI makes the principles of the common good and social justice fundamental criteria for the distribution of goods, wealth, and income, including income from work (57–58). This is manifested concretely in the Pope's attitude toward property. Pope Pius XI emphasizes the dual dimension of property: the individual and the social. In addition to the encyclical "Rerum novarum," in which Leo XIII emphasized the individual right to property for every person, Pius XI points out that the owner must consider not only their own interests but also the common good (45). Determining responsibilities regarding the common good falls within the jurisdiction of the state.[12] Furthermore, Pius XI emphasizes the need to distinguish between the right to property and the right to use property. The Pope rejects the assertion that these are the same rights. The foundation of the former is commutative justice. The use relationship, on the other hand, is associated with other virtues whose exercise cannot be pursued through legal action. This also implies that one does not lose the right to property, even if, as a rightful owner, they do not use or misuse something (47).

Not only private property but also labor has its own individual and social dimensions. From this dual nature of labor, three basic principles that should be considered when determining fair compensation emerge. Payment is just when it is neither too low nor too high. On the one hand, the wage should be sufficient to secure the livelihood of the worker and their family, but on the other hand, it should not be so high as to jeopardize the existence of a well-functioning

based on the idea of the corporate system, was not put into practice. See Firer Hinze (2005, p. 171).

11 Cf. Piwowarczyk (1946).

12 Cf. Firer Hinze (2005, p. 157)

business. Wages must also serve the common good, meaning they must be set in a way that allows as many people as possible to work and live honestly (69–74).

Thirdly, the issue of wages is closely related to the prices of the products sold. Here, too, the Pope emphasizes that both prices and wages should be in the right proportion to each other. This applies not only to individual businesses but also to the overall economy, including various sectors (75).

Regarding private incomes that exceed a reasonable standard of living, Pope Pius XI points out that their use is not a matter of complete freedom but is restricted by the obligation of charity, benevolence, and generosity. In particular, the Pope recommends using these incomes to create jobs that produce useful products (50–51).

The Pope's reference to changes in the capitalist system, which have occurred from the time of Leo XIII to his contemporaries, is very interesting. According to the Pope, the scope of the capitalist economic system has expanded in recent decades. This has taken both a positive and a negative form. Among the negative forms, the Pope places particular emphasis on unlimited economic freedom, which over time has transformed into an economic dictatorship (or the domination of the economy). This is achieved, especially through the concentration of power in the hands of the owners and managers of capital. The Pope particularly points to banks (credit institutions), which, through their activities "(…) regulate the flow, so to speak, of the life-blood whereby the entire economic system lives, and have so firmly in their grasp the soul, as it were, of economic life that no one can breathe against their will" (106).

The Pope criticizes the concentration of power and wealth in the hands of a few, as he believes it leads to conflicts and struggles on multiple levels: firstly, among individuals, secondly, to take control of a state's economic life, and thirdly, to take over the state and make it an instrument in the hands of the rich. Ultimately, this leads to a struggle between states, in which the Pope sees two phenomena: on one side, economic nationalism and economic imperialism. It seems that the Pope is concerned that the wealthy are only looking out for their own interests, even at the expense of others, including foreigners. On the other hand, financial internationalism and international financial imperialism can be identified, which do not consider the interests of the state and its citizens but feel comfortable where they can make money (107–109).

However, the criticism of the dominance of financial institutions cannot be equated with criticism of money itself. Like his predecessor, Pope Pius XI is more concerned with criticizing the misuse of money and demanding that the economic order be based on Christian norms.

3.2.2. "Divini redemptoris"

In the encyclical "Divini Redemptoris," Pope Pius XI rejects the doctrine of atheistic communism as incompatible with the teachings of the Church.[13] In this letter, Pope Pius XI does not directly address money. However, he touches upon the topics of wages and wealth, continuing the thoughts from previous social encyclicals. In the first theme, the Pope refers to the doctrine of fair or just wages. In the second, he reminds the wealthy that wealth is a gift entrusted to them by God to do good. He admonishes them to act according to the principles of commutative and social justice and Christian love, to live modestly, not to seek ultimate happiness on Earth, and not to follow the path of wealth at any cost. He also recognizes the important role of the state in income distribution, as the state's task should be to use its instruments to convince the wealthiest to take responsibility for the common good. This recommendation of the Pope particularly pertains to those who increase their wealth at the expense of others.

3.2.3. "Caritate Christi Compulsi"

Although the encyclical "Caritate Christi Compulsi" by Pope Pius XI is not counted among the Church's social teachings, it is worth mentioning because the Pope included two remarkable thoughts related to the topic of money in it.[14] They correspond to the golden rule cited above, which the Pope established in paragraph 22 of "Rerum Novarum."

Referring to the current situation in the world and with regret, Pius XI points out that some of today's difficulties are related to the economic crisis, including a shortage of money (2). At the same time, the Pope sees the "root of all evils," including the causes of the then crisis, in desire of money (1 Timothy 6:10).[15] From this arises selfishness, which seeks only personal gain and creates social relationships based solely on this motive. The manifestation of these relationships is mutual mistrust, leading to trade restrictions, envy, viewing what others have as a loss for oneself, and ultimately, the concentration of wealth in the hands of a few individuals (3).

---

13 Pius XI (1937).
14 Pius XI (1932).
15 The Greek term φιλαργυρία may refer to love, avarice, greed, desire.

3.3. John XXIII

Pope John XXIII introduces new accents, both in terms of method, the audience, and the content of Catholic social teaching.

3.3.1. "Mater et magistra"

The encyclical "Mater et Magistra" by Pope John XXIII inaugurates a new era in the social teachings of the popes.[16] It is noteworthy for introducing not only new content but also a new tone (openness and optimism from Pope John XXIII) and a new methodology.[17] Pope John XXIII begins his writing with two sentences that can be considered the foundation of the Church's social teachings. They read: "Mother and Teacher of all nations—such is the Catholic Church in the mind of her Founder, Jesus Christ; to hold the world in an embrace of love, that men, in every age, should find in her their own completeness in a higher order of living, and their ultimate salvation" (1).

The Pope makes it clear that the Church's concern, in addition to salvation, also extends to the temporal life of humans, meaning their daily needs, what is necessary for life, and what can be considered wealth and well-being according to the requirements of each era (3). The place wealth should occupy in human life is explained by the Pope as follows: "Certainly, the Church teaches—and has always taught—that scientific and technical progress and the resultant material well-being are good things and mark an important phase in human civilization. But the Church teaches, too, that goods of this kind must be valued according to their true nature: as instruments used by man for the better attainment of his end. They help to make him a better man, both in the natural and the supernatural order" (246).

Thus, wealth itself is not inherently bad as long as it is not given absolute value and is not considered an end but a means of human action. Furthermore, when properly understood, wealth can serve the true development of humanity.

To demonstrate the continuity of the Church's social teachings, John XXIII refers in the first part of his encyclical directly to the most important ideas contained in two previous fundamental documents, namely "Rerum Novarum" and "Quadragesimo Anno."

One of the themes from earlier social teachings is the question of just remuneration. John XXIII revisits this topic. The Pope reminds that wage determination

16 John XXIII (1961).
17 Cf. Mich (2005b, pp. 196–198).

cannot solely rely on market principles or be the arbitrary decision of the stronger contracting party. It must consider the principles of fairness and justice, meaning that the wage should cover the costs necessary for both the worker and their family to maintain a decent standard of living. The Pope emphasizes the importance that all social strata benefit from economic development. He particularly recommends that financially sustainable companies, those making profits, should share these with their employees, especially in companies with minimum wage levels. On the other hand, wage increases should not come at the expense of the common good. In general, it can be concluded that the criteria for determining fair compensation for labor should consider the actual capacity of the worker, the financial situation of the company, the well-being of the nation, and the requirements of the common good for all nations (71–78, 112). It's essential to note that the consideration of the requirements of the common good, both on a national and international level, applies not only to workers or the poorest but also to entrepreneurs, who may rightfully claim a fair share of the profits generated, and to capital providers who should be entitled to dividends (81).

Concerning other topics, it can be posited that John XXIII's fundamental idea is that social and economic actions should lead to the elimination or at least reduction of differences between individuals, industries, and ultimately nations. Here, the Pope sees the vital role of the state.

In the Pope's view, the state should pursue an economic and social policy that allows as broad access to private property, including stakes in companies, as possible (115). Regarding the specific state authorities of a given country, the Pope calls for their involvement in creating mechanisms serving this purpose. Here, the Pope pays particular attention to agriculture and underdeveloped regions. According to the Pope, the instruments under the state's jurisdiction include appropriate wage, price, tax, credit, and investment policies. State involvement should be based on the principles of the common good and subsidiarity. This means that the state should only do what contributes to the common benefit of its citizens, supports their own efforts to improve their condition, and encourages other private institutions, especially entrepreneurs and capital providers, to actively participate in the country's development (150–152).

Specific topics mentioned here that deserve attention include a just tax system, price regulation in agriculture, insurance for the agricultural sector, and public credit allocation.

The principle of justice and fairness should be the basis for a just tax system. Such a system should be designed so that tax burdens are adjusted to the financial capabilities of citizens and consider the specifics of their employment (e.g., in agriculture) (132–133).

John XXIII advocates for price regulation of agricultural products. The Pope argues that it would be most appropriate if prices were determined based on market mechanisms, but the peculiarity of agriculture requires state intervention. Prices for agricultural products should be low enough for everyone to afford them, while also ensuring farmers receive a decent income. The Pope does not provide concrete solutions, whether state intervention should come in the form of suitable legal regulations or some form of agricultural subsidies. Regarding prices for agricultural products, the Pope believes that prices should give greater consideration to compensating the work of the farmer rather than the costs of borrowed money (137–141).

In an analysis of the role of financial institutions, the Pope mentions credit and insurance activities. John XXIII notes that not only private but also public institutions are capital providers.

Pope John XXIII seems to affirm the insurance and social insurance system. However, here too, adjustment to the principles of justice and fairness is necessary. This means, for example, that all social and occupational groups should have access to a similar range of insurance and social benefits. The system should not be diversified based on the incomes of the insured, as this would create unfavorable conditions for poorer people. The Pope demands that the insurance and social insurance system be an instrument for reducing class differences in society.[18] One of the practical solutions proposed by the Pope is the need to create two insurance systems for agriculture: one for the farmers themselves and another for the yields of their work (135–136).

John XXIII believes that credit policy is one of the state's responsibilities. In the encyclical, the Pope elaborates on this idea when presenting his requirements for economic policy concerning agriculture. Income in agriculture is generated more slowly and with greater risk, making it difficult for farmers to obtain the necessary financial resources. Therefore, the common good demands that the state pursues a special credit policy and establishes specialized banks that provide low-interest cash loans to farmers (88, 134).

Finally, when considering domestic matters, it should be mentioned that the principles of the common good and subsidiarity apply not only to national policy but also to the international sphere. The Pope thanks international financial

---

18 According to the Pope, the role of property changes in the era of insurance and social security systems, meaning that it is no longer necessary as a future security. This is also related to the fact that today's people value income from work more than profits and rights from capital (105–106).

institutions and wealthy countries for the aid they provide to poor nations. At the same time, he reminds the wealthy nations of their duty and requests further support for the development of poorer nations. This support should be facilitated, among other things, by easing international trade, the movement of people and capital (155–157, 163, 165).

In addition to the areas mentioned above, where the Pope indirectly addresses the topic of money, there is a passage in the encyclical where money's value is directly referenced, specifically the need to maintain a stable price level.

As part of the call to support the technical development of agriculture, the Pope makes an important contribution. One of the essential prerequisites for economic development, in his view, is the preservation of the purchasing power of money. Interestingly, according to the Pope, this price stability should be achieved through better alignment of supply and demand in trade between agriculture, services, and industry, as well as through improved adaptation of supply to consumer demand. However, the Pope does not further elaborate on this idea. Therefore, it is not known whether, in his opinion, the mismatch between supply and demand in the economy only affects economic growth or is one of the sources of instability in purchasing power. One thing seems clear to the Pope, though: the stability of the purchasing power of money is a value (129).

3.3.2. "Pacem in terris"

In the title of the encyclical "Pacem in Terris," Pope John XXIII already indicates that its content is peace among nations, founded on truth, justice, love, and freedom.[19] The encyclical does not directly address the topic of money. The Pope only mentions the right of every worker to a salary in accordance with the principles of justice and fairness, that is, a salary that allows them and their family to live a dignified life within the available means. The guarantor for such a wage should be the state (23–24, 64). In describing the duties of the state, the Pope notes that this includes the creation of an insurance system that ensures an adequate standard of living for people who are victims of accidents or family circumstances that deprive them of the possibility of such a life. Finally, the Pope reaffirms the teachings of his predecessors regarding international relations, including the proposal to facilitate international capital flows (101).

19 John XXIII (1963).

3.4. Paul VI and His Encyclical "Populorum Progressio"

"Populorum progressio" by Paul VI is one of the most important social encyclicals of the 20th century.[20] It contains, like other previous social encyclicals, a number of references to the individual and social dimensions of economic life, but also fails to address the issue of money directly. Money is only an indirect theme here, its significance derived from other economic issues raised in the encyclical.

The main theme of the encyclical written by Pope Paul VI in 1967 is the development of people.[21] Development is essential because, as emphasized by Paul VI, it is synonymous with peace. The Pope advocates for "genuine progress and true development" meaning an economy in the service of humanity, providing daily bread for all. Such development contributes to brotherhood of men and demonstrates the working of Divine Providence. The concept of brotherhood is one of the foundations of the papal understanding of the ethical basis of economic relationships (86–87).

Pope Paul VI examines the relationship between the rich and the poor on both the individual (personal) and collective (national) levels. The moral responsibility for the fate of others, according to the Pope, arises from the human and supernatural brotherhood of people. This principle is grounded in three types of duties: the duty of mutual solidarity, social justice, and love for all people (universal charity). These duties include richer nations assisting poorer nations, improving economic relations between stronger and weaker nations, and building a community of people where the progress of some does not come at the expense of others. From this principle, it follows that the wealth one possesses should not be used solely for one's benefit but should also serve the welfare of others (44–49). In other words, by invoking the principle of brotherhood, Paul VI confirms and reminds us of the Church's teaching that the right to private property is not absolute. Those who have abundance are obligated to share with those who lack what is necessary for life (23).

---

20 Paul VI (1967).

21 Deck calls this encyclical a "magna carta on development". The Pope uses the term "development," referring to its social and economic dimension, and tries to connect it with the Christian understanding of the human person. Deck argues that in the encyclical Paul VI reversed the position of his predecessors on the topic of private property. Instead of emphasizing individual rights, as before, the social function of property takes precedence. See Deck (2005, p. 300).

Building on this principle, Paul VI concludes that the duty of brotherhood extends to all people and all nations, to every rich person and every person in need. In this context, the Pope poses some specific questions to contemporary individuals. He asks whether people are willing to support, at their own expense, works and tasks for the poor, pay higher taxes for development, pay higher prices for imported goods to ensure decent wages for producers, and, if necessary, leave their homeland at a young age to help emerging nations (47).

In paragraph 21 of the encyclical, the Pope distinguishes between what is less human and what is more human. The first group includes the lack of a minimum standard of living, violent state structures resulting from abuse of property or power, exploitation of workers, or unfair business practices. Conversely, more humane conditions can be achieved, including the possession of life's necessities (21).

However, not every effort to acquire goods is good. Pope Paul VI distinguishes between legitimate and distorted human desires for possession. Recognizing that human development also requires a certain level of material security, the Pope affirms the pursuit of necessary goods. At the same time, he warns against greed: "But the acquisition of worldly goods can lead men to greed, to the unrelenting desire for more, to the pursuit of greater personal power. Rich and poor alike—be they individuals, families or nations—can fall prey to avarice and soulstifling materialism" (18).

Greed can threaten anyone, whether rich or poor, individuals or entire nations. The Pope notes that those infected by greed are morally underdeveloped. Furthermore, greed leads to materialism, which is a threat to spiritual development. The Pope writes, "(…) the exclusive pursuit of material possessions prevents man's growth as a human being and stands in opposition to his true grandeur" (19).

Paul VI extends the teaching from the encyclical "Rerum Novarum" on the just wage to international agreements. In this context, the Pope criticizes economic relationships based solely on the law of free and unrestricted competition, as this often leads to economic dictatorship. International trade and economic relations based on free market principles can only benefit both parties when they resemble each other in terms of prosperity. When the parties to an agreement are characterized by unequal bargaining power, the rules of the free market fail because they can be used by the stronger party to impose unfair conditions. This makes the rich richer and the poor poorer. In such cases, both contracting parties should be guided by the principle of brotherhood. It should be emphasized that the Pope is not advocating for the abolition of competition and the principles of the free market but rather their regulation within limits that do not violate the principles of justice and human dignity (57–61).

Paul VI's teaching on trade relationships based on the principle of brotherhood has another essential dimension. Unfair trade relationships can undermine efforts, in the form of financial and technical assistance, to support poorer countries. Therefore, the Pope advocates for dialogue between aid recipients and donors. The purpose of such dialogue is to avoid the danger of donated or loaned money becoming an instrument of pressure and the imposition of the particular interests of the rich rather than a tool for helping and building the international community (54–56).

In paragraph 54 of the encyclical, the Pope specifies what the subject of dialogue should be. It first concerns the amount of available aid on the one hand and the actual need and the possibility of effectively using these resources on the other. Furthermore, the specific parameters of the loans to be granted, such as the interest rate and repayment terms, should be agreed upon so that loan repayment is possible and does not lead to the debtor's overindebtedness. The lender has the right to expect that the money is used reasonably but cannot connect the granting of a loan with the right to interfere in the internal affairs of the borrowing country. This dialogue should lead to an agreement guaranteeing the creation of an international community respecting human dignity (54). One of the concrete proposals put forward in the encyclical is a renewed appeal to those in power to use a portion of their military spending to create a fund to support the poor (51).[22]

Apart from the emphasized points above, the theme of money indirectly appears in some other parts of the encyclical, which are briefly mentioned here.

Paul VI points out that work can have a dark side, as it can stimulate egoism and even revolt by promising money, pleasure, and power. However, it is not clear what role money itself plays in triggering these negative attitudes or behaviors, and what significance other motives may have (28).

Elsewhere, the Pope notes that the only path to peace is through civilizational and economic development. Therefore, his appeal to the business world to not be guided solely by their own interests but also to initiate measures for social progress and human advancement is understandable (70, 83).

Referring to the Second Vatican Council's Constitution "Gaudium et Spes," Paul VI strongly rejects the practices of those who invest income earned in their

22 Such an appeal was first made by Paul VI on December 4, 1964, in a speech to journalists in Mumbai. See Paul VI (1964).

country abroad, solely driven by their own interests rather than the interests of their own country (24).

In his critique of one form of liberalism, which Paul VI describes as unbridled liberalism, he refers to the words from the encyclical "Quadragesimo Anno" regarding financial internationalism or international financial imperialism. However, the Pope does not further develop this thread (26).

3.5. Pope John Paul II

Pope John Paul II. provided significant impulses for the adaptation of Catholic social teaching to the new situation.

3.5.1. "Laborem exercens"

Pope John Paul II. commemorated the 90th anniversary of the encyclical "Rerum novarum" by issuing the encyclical "Laborem exercens."[23] This encyclical is one of those papal teaching documents that address a topic from multiple perspectives.[24] The theme of labor is among the most important in the Church's teaching, which is reflected in practically every document of Catholic social doctrine. This is also due to the fact that the Church understands itself and its mission as "the Church of the poor." Who is the poor? According to John Paul II, the poor appear in many forms, in various places, and at different times. Among the reasons for poverty is unemployment or wages falling below just compensation (8). According to the Pope, the criterion for whether a particular socio-economic system is just, that is, whether it functions justly, lies in how work is appropriately remunerated in such a system (19).

Although money itself is not directly addressed by the Pope, there is a close relationship between money and labor. This relationship manifests itself in the payment of the worker. John Paul II defines the just wage of a worker, on whose shoulders the support of a family should rest, as sufficient for the establishment, maintenance, and security of that family's future.[25] According to the Pope, a just wage can take two forms. The first is the so-called family-supporting wage,

---

23 John Paul II (1981).

24 This group also includes e.g. Paul VI (1967) or Pope Francis (2015).

25 According to Lamoureux, the concept of the family wage is a historically conditioned construct that includes gender-based inequalities and a patriarchal perception of the family, where the man is responsible for the family's livelihood, and the woman is responsible for the care of the home and children. See Lamoureux (2005, p. 401).

where the head of the family earns enough that the spouse is not forced into outside employment. The second form of just compensation includes special social benefits such as family allowances or maternity benefits. Furthermore, the Pope notes that such just remuneration does not exhaust all the rights of workers, especially because they have the right to vacation, retirement, old-age security, or accident insurance (19).[26]

How is an agreement reached on the wage level? According to the words of John Paul II, three actors participate in wage formation: the indirect employer who creates the framework for specific contracts between the direct employer, that is, the one employing a particular worker, and the worker themselves. The framework created by the indirect employer allows the direct employer to offer fair compensation or to pay less than the objective requirements of the workers would dictate (11–12). Pope John Paul II defines the indirect employer as "(...) all the agents at the national and international level that are responsible for the whole orientation of labour policy" (18). For the Pope, the instances he calls the "indirect employer" are the people, institutions, and conditions that determine the socio-economic order, including the rules of the labor market (17). For the Pope, remuneration is thus not purely private; it is not just an agreement between two entities but, like labor itself, it is social. Besides compensation, two other topics deserve attention: capital and private property.

John Paul II refers to the term "capital" in two senses. The Pope nowhere in the encyclical refers to financial capital but only to material capital. By capital, John Paul II understands the totality of the means of production and, in a narrower sense, the sum of things. Capital consists of natural resources available to humans and products of human labor, through which humans adapt natural resources to their own needs. In the second—historical—sense, the term "capital" refers to a small but influential group of people who own the means of production and as such stand in opposition to the working class (11–12). The Pope recalls the teaching that the Catholic Church does not view the right to property as an absolute right but conceives it within the framework of the universal destination of goods, that is, the universal purpose of goods. Furthermore, John Paul II emphasizes that property must not be used against labor (14).

26 This is the strongest statement in Catholic social teaching about just work. Cf. Lamoureux (2005, p. 400).

3.5.2. "Centesimus annus"

Exactly a hundred years after "Rerum novarum," Pope John Paul II's social encyclical "Centesimus Annus" was published.[27] As with previous documents commemorating Leo XIII's encyclical, the aim here is to recall and update the teachings of "Rerum novarum."

The topic of money itself does not appear in the encyclical "Centesimus annus" at all. However, the Pope indirectly refers to money, especially when addressing the economy. These considerations are based on the doctrine of property rights and the universal destination of goods. The starting point is the question of the origin of goods that serve humans in sustaining life, satisfying their needs, and being the subject of their rights. In response, the Pope emphasizes the importance of human labor and highlights the value of economic activity.[28] John Paul II expresses this with the following words: "The modern business economy has positive aspects. Its basis is human freedom exercised in the economic field, just as it is exercised in many other fields. Economic activity is indeed but one sector in a great variety of human activities, and like every other sector, it includes the right to freedom, as well as the duty of making responsible use of freedom" (32).

The freedom of economic activity also implies the recognition of a certain degree of autonomy in the relationship between the economy and the state, that is, an area in which the state should not intervene (15).[29] However, recognizing the positive dimension of economic life does not mean that the Pope views it unilaterally or even absolutizes it. The Pope is aware of the inadequacies of the economy; for instance, he describes capital, citing the encyclical "Rerum novarum," as a new form of property (4), which, in a simplified form, conflicts with labor (5, 6). Elsewhere, he mentions that in the earliest phase of capitalism, there was, and may still be, a form of this system in which there is "inhuman exploitation" (33).[30] In general, it is unacceptable to have an economic system where capital, ownership of production tools and land, has absolute dominion over the free subjectivity of human labor (35).

If one understands the modern economy as a market economy, it is unimaginable without money. Where there is a market, there is also money. Therefore,

---

27 John Paul II (1991).

28 When the Pope speaks of wealth, he refers to work and also to human labor as its main factors (31).

29 However, it is the responsibility of the state to regulate and engage in economic policy where the economy and the market cannot guarantee adequate solutions (15).

30 Interestingly, the Pope refers to socialism as State capitalism (35).

it seems that the way the Popes understand and evaluate the market can also be applied to money. In the encyclical "Centesimus annus," John Paul II writes: "[O] n the level of individual nations and of international relations, the free market is the most efficient instrument for utilizing resources and effectively responding to needs. But this is true only for those needs which are 'solvent', insofar as they are endowed with purchasing power, and for those resources which are 'marketable', insofar as they are capable of obtaining a satisfactory price. But there are many human needs which find no place on the market" (34).[31]

The market is a tool through which resources can be better utilized, the exchange of products is facilitated, and needs can be met through voluntary exchange. By emphasizing the importance and value of the market, the Pope also opposes its absolutist understanding. He emphasizes that the market has limits, creating those individual and social needs that cannot be met through exchange and market mechanisms. Ignoring this, the Pope warns, carries the danger of idolizing the market, that is, the risk of it becoming a form of idolatry (40).

With the acceptance of the economy and the market also comes the acceptance of profit. The Church acknowledges the positive role of profit. Profit is a determining factor and a measure of the proper functioning of a business, that is, the proper utilization of production and manufacturing factors and the offering of products that meet human needs. Of course, profit cannot be the sole criterion for assessing economic activity. Alongside profit, human and moral factors must also be considered. In this context, the Pope makes an important point. In his view, a company that does not operate on moral principles cannot survive in the long run because it represents a community of people "(…) who in various ways are endeavouring to satisfy their basic needs, and who form a particular group at the service of the whole of society" (35).[32]

Similarly, the Pope assesses the ownership of means of production. This right is not absolute, whether it concerns means of production in industry or agriculture. The Pope emphasizes that such ownership is only justified when it serves useful work. Conversely, if it is not productive, hinders the work of others, or

---

31 The Pope does not define how he understands the "free market." The "market" itself seems to be associated with capitalism as a form of social and economic system opposed to Marxism (34).

32 Finn points out that John Paul II shifts the focus "from the right *of* private property toward the right *to* private property" (italics D.F.). The right to private property belongs to anyone who has to provide for themselves and their family, not just those who actually own property (2005, p. 446).

serves to generate income through exploitation or speculation, it is unlawful. The Pope states emphatically: "Ownership of this kind has no justification, and represents an abuse in the sight of God and man" (43).

So what is the papal vision of the place of the economy or the market in the lives of people and nations? It points to a social order based on the principles of labor freedom, entrepreneurship, and participation (35). At the same time, it is an order in which economic freedom is not understood as an absolute value but serves full human freedom (42). In such an order, the market has its place, but there are also market regulatory mechanisms and those that, in a non-market manner, through state economic policy, enable the satisfaction of the basic needs of the entire society (35). Among the tasks of the state in such a world is the provision of so-called public goods that are not market goods, including the protection of the natural and human environment (40).

Regarding specific topics related to money, the Pope mentions credit cooperatives (16), which have developed as a result of the Church's social teaching, among other factors. He also refers to the foreign debt of poor countries. The Pope does not fundamentally question that debts must be repaid. However, this principle should not be absolute. The poorest countries cannot be required to pay their debts at the cost of excessive sacrifices, particularly hunger and desperation. The fundamental right of every nation is the right to existence and progress. While preserving this right, ways to solve the debt problem of poor countries should be sought, which may include reducing, deferring, or even canceling all debts (35).

Finally, the Pope also addresses investments. John Paul II starts from the premise that the desire for a better life is not a bad thing unless the desire for more hinders personal development (the possibility to be more). This criterion should be applied to consumption, saving, and investments. According to the Pope, investing means giving "(…) people an opportunity to make good use of their own labour" (36). This is not only an economic decision but also a moral and cultural one.

3.5.3. "Sollicitudo rei socialis"

In recognition of the special significance of Pope Paul VI's encyclical "Populorum progressio," Pope John Paul II, on the twentieth anniversary of its creation, released the encyclical "Sollicitudo rei socialis."[33] As with every jubilee encyclical,

33 John Paul II (1987).

the goal of the 1987 document is twofold: to honor the work of his predecessor and to promote theological reflection on current reality, emphasizing both the continuity and the ongoing renewal of the Church's social doctrine (3–4). "Sollicitudo rei socialis" strengthened the concept of solidarity, making it a central and fundamental element of the Church's social doctrine.[34]

While characterizing the contribution of the encyclical "Populorum progressio" to the Church's social doctrine, John Paul II points out that his predecessor addressed the moral dimension of the social question. The duty of solidarity is a moral obligation, meaning that decision-makers in wealthy countries have a moral duty to consider the consequences of their decisions on the suffering and underdevelopment of other people or nations (9). In paragraph 37 of the encyclical, the Pope states that the source of evil hindering the true development of nations is not of an economic nature but rather "a moral evil, the fruit of many sins which lead to 'structures of sin.'" Elsewhere, the Pope writes, "The principal obstacle to be overcome on the way to authentic liberation is sin and the structures produced by sin as it multiplies and spreads" (46) In this way, John Paul II continues the thought of Paul VI and enriches the analysis of socio-political relationships with a religious dimension. The Pope explains that his aim is to present a broader perspective, placing social relationships in the context of God's will and plan for humanity. Actions and behaviors that run counter to God's will and the well-being of others and contribute to the formation of "structures of sin" include, according to the Pope, the exclusive pursuit of profit at any cost and the pursuit of power at any cost. The Pope refers to these attitudes as a "double attitude of sin" (37). According to the Pope, these attitudes manifest themselves, for example, in decisions motivated by the idolatry of money, ideology, class, or technology, which only seem to be based on economic or political reasons (28). It seems that John Paul II understands "structures of sin" as collective situations or behaviors, which he referred to in the post-synodal apostolic exhortation "Reconciliatio et paenitentia" as "social sin," and here in "Sollicitudo rei socialis," he defines them as "[t]he sum total of the negative factors working against a true awareness of the universal common good, and the need to further it, gives the impression of creating, in persons and institutions, an obstacle which is difficult to overcome" (36).[35]

34 For more on this topic, see, e.g., Curran et al. (2005, pp. 426–430).

35 In his apostolic exhortation "Reconciliatio et paenitentia," John Paul II addresses the issue of social sin. The starting point, however, is personal sin. The Pope explains that "[s]in, in the proper sense, is always a personal act, since it is an act of freedom on the part of an individual person and not properly of a group or community." Following

Referring to the Second Vatican Council's constitution "Gaudium et spes," John Paul II distinguishes between "having" and "being," with "being" meaning the "realization of human vocation." "Having" is not inherently bad, but the disorderly form of having is criticized by the Pope. John Paul II writes: "The evil does not consist in 'having' as such, but in possessing without regard for the quality and the hierarchy of the goods one has. Quality and hierarchy arise from the subordination of goods and their availability to man's 'being' and his true vocation" (28).

The Pope draws attention to two phenomena in the modern world. On the one hand, there are underdeveloped and poor regions, and on the other hand, there are areas where there is overdevelopment, characterized by a civilization of "consumption" or consumerism, which is characterized by the cult of "having." So which form of "having" is affirmed? The text suggests an understanding of possession that does not lead to the enslavement of people but is guided by moral principles and directed toward the well-being of humanity, contributing to the perfection of individuals, that is, the realization of their "being," and the just distribution of goods or services originally intended for all of humanity (28).

In the context of the hierarchy of values and the relationship between "being" and "having," the Pope reminds Christians that it is the duty of each of them to help the poor, not only with excess but also from what is necessary, especially

---

this introduction, the Pope distinguishes three meanings of the term "social sin." Such a sin is: (a) Any sin of any person because it somehow harms others, i.e., the Church and the whole world; (b) Sin against the neighbor, especially against love, individual justice, or justice in the relationship between the individual and the community, against the rights of the human person, against the common good and its requirements. This group also includes sins committed by political, economic, and trade union leaders, as well as by workers in professional relationships, either by action or by negligence; (c) Sins committed in relations between different communities. The Pope mentions class struggle, conflicts between various interest groups within states, between states, and even blocs of states. Although the Pope calls certain forms of social sin sins in an analogous sense because sometimes it is difficult to attribute moral responsibility to a specific person, this by no means weakens or negates the personal responsibility of the individual here. John Paul II emphasizes: "Whenever the church speaks of situations of sin or when the condemns as social sins certain situations or the collective behavior of certain social groups, big or small, or even of whole nations and blocs of nations, she knows and she proclaims that such cases of social sin are the result of the accumulation and concentration of many personal sins. (…) A situation-or likewise an institution, a structure, society itself-is not in itself the subject of moral acts. Hence a situation cannot in itself be good or bad" (1984, no. 16).

when the "having" of some comes at the expense of the "being" of others.[36] The Pope gives the example that in some situations, it may be necessary to sell valuable items from the church's furnishings and donate the funds to the needy (31).

Regarding wealth and poverty, John Paul II refers to the conventional division between the rich North and the underdeveloped South. At the same time, the Pope points out that the problem of wealth and poverty is not limited to differences between countries. Even within rich countries, there are areas of poverty, and in less developed countries, there are signs of egoism and displays of wealth (14). It is essential to mention that the Pope adheres to the diagnosis of his predecessors and understands poverty comprehensively. In addition to economic underdevelopment, there is also cultural, political, and simply human underdevelopment (15).

The duty to care for the poor can also be derived from the papal understanding of property. The Catholic Church considers the right to private property to be correct and necessary but opposes understanding it as an absolute right. The pastoral constitution "Gaudium et spes" emphasizes the principle of the universal destination of goods. According to Pope John Paul II, property carries a "social mortgage," which means that the social function is an inherent quality of property (42).

How does what has been said about the poor and property relate to international relations? First, it should be noted that John Paul II encourages nations in the same geographical zones to strengthen economic cooperation to make their economies more independent.[37] Such cooperation could include the currency and financial sector. However, the Pope does not specify the concrete forms of such cooperation, especially the instruments it would require (42).

Then the Pope addresses the question of the use of funds at the international level. Financial and investment assistance to poorer countries should be aimed at supporting their development. However, there are cases where this assistance does not serve development but goes against the interests of the recipient countries and is even used to fuel conflicts in those countries. Furthermore, financial support is sometimes tied to the implementation of ideological demands imposed on poorer countries, such as birth control campaigns. In the Pope's

36 "[O]ption or love of preference for the poor" means "an option, or a special form of primacy in the exercise of Christian charity" (42).

37 The Pope does not specify exactly which zones he means. Previously, he wrote generally about North and South, as well as East and West (24).

view, this is nothing more than a new form of violence being exerted on these countries.

Another area where the use of money is morally questionable and can lead "towards death" is the financing of weapons production and trade. This is especially concerning since the arms trade, unlike other areas of economic relations between states, is subject to no controls or restrictions. It also happens that weapons are purchased with funds provided by rich countries (21, 23–25).

Regarding money and the mechanisms for its management, the criticism presented by John Paul II in paragraph 16 of the encyclical is important. The Pope writes: "[O]ne must denounce the existence of economic, financial and social mechanisms which, although they are manipulated by people, often function almost automatically, thus accentuating the situation of wealth for some and poverty for the rest. These mechanisms, which are maneuvered directly or indirectly by the more developed countries, by their very functioning favor the interests of the people manipulating them at in the end they suffocate or condition the economies of the less developed countries" (16).

It is not clear which mechanisms John Paul II exactly has in mind. When describing signs of underdevelopment in poorer countries, the Pope mentions international debt as one of them, and in this context he returns to the topic of these mechanisms. The granting and acceptance of loans (or, in a broader sense, capital) is, in itself, desirable and correct. However, the Pope continues to write: "Circumstances have changed, both within the debtor nations and in the international financial market; the instrument chosen to make a contribution to development has turned into a counterproductive mechanism" (19).

In other words, instead of supporting development, this instrument or mechanism contributes to inhibiting development or exacerbating underdevelopment. What are the symptoms of a negative impact of such an instrument? The Pope mentions two: the lack of access to new funds and the need to service foreign debts with funds necessary to increase or maintain the living standards in poorer countries (19).

It appears that the Pope had in mind the global escalation of financial crises that occurred in the late 1970s and especially in the early 1980s, accompanied by an increase in exchange rate volatility and interest rates. This can be confirmed by the following sentence: "The world monetary and financial system is marked by an excessive fluctuation of exchange rates and interest rates, to the detriment of the balance of payments and the debt situation of the poorer countries" (43). In this statement, the Pope apparently refers to the increase in interest rates and the strengthening of currencies in which rich countries and international institutions lend money to poor countries. It remains unclear whether such an increase is justified and what the justification for it is. In other words, is it the result of a market mechanism, that is, the effect of risk in the market, or is it a conscious action by someone? And, finally, is usury being discussed here?

3.6. Benedict XVI and His Encyclical "Caritas in Veritate"

To honor Paul VI, and to recall and update the encyclical "Populorum progressio," Pope Benedict XVI wrote the encyclical "Caritas in veritate."[38] Benedict XVI emphasized the significance of his predecessor's encyclical with the following words: "I express my conviction that Populorum Progressio deserves to be considered 'the Rerum Novarum of the present age', shedding light upon humanity's journey towards unity" (8). Another important factor in the composition of the encyclical was the economic and financial crisis and the ongoing process of globalization. The Pope acknowledged the benefits of globalization but did not turn a blind eye to the challenges and threats it posed to individuals and societies (42).

In reference to his contemporary era, Benedict XVI noted that economic progress has been a positive factor in human development. For example, he argued that this progress has contributed to lifting billions of people out of poverty (21). However, the overall economic growth of the world, often seen as an increase in wealth, has not eliminated the problem of inequality and poverty. Hence, the repeated calls by many popes to address this issue. Benedict XVI pointed out several negative phenomena in this context, including excessive and consumption-oriented development by a few groups of people, corruption, lawlessness, violation of labor rights by local and international companies, and inappropriate international aid (22).

One of the main themes of the encyclical is the market economy. As the name suggests, it is based on the market. To understand the essence of market-based economic activity, including the concept of money, it is crucial to understand how the market itself is understood. In paragraph 35 of the encyclical, Benedict XVI presents his own understanding of the market and that of Catholic social teaching, leading to the following definition of the market: "In a climate of mutual trust, the market is the economic institution that permits encounter between persons, inasmuch as they are economic subjects who make use of contracts to regulate their relations as they exchange goods and services of equivalent value between them, in order to satisfy their needs and desires" (35).

38 Benedict XVI (2009).

The Pope noted that the market is relevant to one area of human activity, namely the economy. Like the economy itself, the market is a social institution in the sense that it enables the interaction of people. The market serves humanity because it enables individuals to satisfy their needs and desires. This satisfaction is based on the principle of commutative justice, which means that mutual and general trust must exist, exchanges must be regulated on a contractual basis, and the parties involved in the exchange must be equal.

At the same time, the Pope recognized that the market, which—when exchanging goods—is guided solely by the principle of equivalence of their value, cannot achieve social unity, a unity without which it cannot function well in return.[39] Benedict XVI recalled the social teaching of the Church, emphasizing that distributive justice and social justice are important for the market economy. Therefore, the market, with its commutative justice, is not absolute and "must draw its moral energies from other subjects that are capable of generating them" (35).

Does this mean that the market itself is bad? The Pope understands that the market is just a tool, which means that it is neither inherently good nor bad. However, like any tool, the market can be abused, for example, as a site of violence by the strong against the weak. Human selfishness, a clouded human mind, false ideologies, or cultures can shape market relationships. In other words, economic activity, like any human activity, has moral consequences and should therefore be structured and institutionalized ethically. As the Pope rightly notes, "Therefore it is not the instrument that must be called to account, but individuals, their moral conscience and their personal and social responsibility" (36).

For Benedict XVI, this also means that the logic of the market should coexist with the political logic and the logic of gift without reciprocity. It is not about the autonomy of each of them but about their interaction.[40] By political logic, the Pope means both the right and duty of political authority to enact laws that ensure that the principles of commutative justice are respected by every market participant and the responsibility of the state to conduct redistribution policies based on norms of commutative justice. In this regard, the introduction of the

39 With this, the Pope seems to understand the end of social conflicts and the reign of mutual trust.

40 As Krucina notes, the Pope sees the reformation of the current situation as a great task for the triangle of State—Market—Civil Society. Assuming that these three dimensions are coordinated to create a certain moral space, the Pope also sees the need to develop a market economy. See Krucina (2010, pp. 158–162).

principle of so-called fiscal subsidiarity could be helpful, meaning that the state could allow citizens to decide on the use of the taxes they pay (60). The logic of gratuitous gift, on the other hand, refers to economic initiatives that, in their business activities, pursue goals other than profit, that is, those that prioritize people.[41] The Pope particularly has in mind a form of business that shapes profit as a means to achieve the goal of a "more human market and society" (36–38, 46–47).[42] In this context, the Pope's words about profit also make sense: "Profit is useful if it serves as a means towards an end that provides a sense both of how to produce it and how to make good use of it. Once profit becomes the exclusive goal, if it is produced by improper means and without the common good as its ultimate end, it risks destroying wealth and creating poverty" (21).

Therefore, if profit is earned fairly and its use corresponds to the common good, then such profit is affirmed within the social doctrine of the Church.[43] The Pope seems to accept the existence of commercial enterprises since he writes about the need for a market where enterprises with various operational objectives, including profit-oriented private enterprises, can operate (38). However, it is not entirely clear how Benedict XVI understands an enterprise itself, especially whether he sees it as an instrument for satisfying human needs in the economic sphere.[44]

The Pope believes that the understanding of enterprises should change as old forms of enterprises disappear and new ones emerge, bringing different risks. At the forefront, the Pope mentions the risk of an enterprise being primarily accountable to investors and thus reducing its social dimension. This is attributed to the increase in the so-called cosmopolitan class of managers who are primarily accountable to shareholders (typically anonymous funds). However, the management of an enterprise should consider the interests of all those who

41 The coexistence of different economic models in the economy is referred to by the Pope as "economic democracy" or "civilizing the economy" (38).

42 Interestingly, the Pope uses utilitarian arguments here because he does not reject the existence of traditional for-profit businesses, but claims that they should be multiple institutional business sectors (the Pope also mentions non-profit organizations) because this diversity contributes to a more humane and at the same time more competitive market.

43 It seems, however, that the common good here is to be understood primarily as one's own good, which does not endanger the good of others. The adequate satisfaction of one's own needs would therefore be compatible with the realization of the common good.

44 For more on this topic, see, e.g., Szewczyk (2020, pp. 115–123).

contribute to its activities, such as employees, customers, suppliers, or the community in which it operates.[45]

The second area that Benedict XVI addresses is the question of investments and capital mobility. Benedict XVI continues the thoughts of his predecessors (Paul VI and John Paul II) and elaborates on this topic. The Pope sees the positive aspects of foreign investments but calls for the avoidance of speculative situations where investments are focused more on short-term gains than on long-term benefits for the enterprise itself. Investments that are exploitative and do not contribute to the development of the local community are also deemed unacceptable (40, 46–47). The primary manifestation of globalization is the increasing mobility of financial capital, means of production, and labor (24). This poses not only economic but also political challenges. The growing global competition that puts social protection of workers under pressure threatens national protection and welfare systems. The Pope seems to have reservations about economic policies that abandon income distribution mechanisms, especially against budget policies aiming to reduce social expenditures (25). In the Pope's view, this requires a reconsideration of the roles of national governments in the face of new challenges. On the international level, Benedict XVI believes that the political response should be the creation of a genuine, universally recognized public authority, a global government (24, 67).[46]

The market consists not only of companies, providers of goods and services, but also of their buyers, the consumers. Benedict XVI observes that a new world power has been created, the power of consumers and their associations. The Pope sees the positive aspects of this phenomenon but also warns of the negative consequences. The consumer must be aware that buying is not just an economic but also a moral act. Therefore, purchasing imposes obligations on the consumer, both to oneself and to others, and entails social responsibility. In this context, Benedict XVI refers to the appeal of John Paul II to educate consumers about responsible consumption.[47] One manifestation of such an attitude is, for example, ensuring that those who produce in poor countries are fairly compensated for their goods.

---

45 All of these are referred to as stakeholders. For more on this topic, see, e.g., Figge & Schaltegger (2000, pp. 11–12).

46 The idea of establishing such an authority is already present in the texts of the Second Vatican Council and in earlier social encyclicals. Cf. Vatican Council II (1965b, no. 81); Paul VI (1967, no. 78); John XXIII (1963, no. 84).

47 Cf. John Paul II (1991, no. 36).

By acknowledging the existence of profit-oriented enterprises, the Pope also seems to accept the existence of financial institutions, including banks. At a general level, the entire economic life is an arena of human activity, and as such, it should be oriented toward people and their well-being. Financial institutions play an important role here, as the funds they provide can enhance the material prosperity of people. Regarding concrete solutions, Benedict XVI appreciates that there are examples of ethical actions and ethical behavior among financial institutions. For instance, some banks offer so-called "ethical" accounts and "ethical" investment funds for account holders, and there are forms of ethical financing for those in need (45).[48]

Benedict XVI continues the appeal of his predecessors to help poorer countries and regions in solidarity. One dimension of this help should be financial support. Such assistance (referred to as "financial plans" by the Pope) should ultimately aim to empower poor countries to satisfy their consumption needs and develop their citizens independently. The effect of such support should also be to facilitate the entry of products from poor countries into international markets and thereby promote the participation of as many actors as possible in world trade.[49] The Pope provides concrete examples of such aid, including investments in rural infrastructure, irrigation systems, transportation, market organization, education, and the dissemination of appropriate agricultural techniques (27–28, 58).

However, Benedict XVI also points out that banks and other financial institutions can have a detrimental impact on the (real) economy when their activities are misused or when they engage in speculation.[50] The question arises as to what the Pope specifically means in both cases (21, 45). Generally, it seems to the Pope that loans may not bring the expected benefits and may even harm borrowers, particularly when it comes to international financial institutions advocating for reductions in social spending. This poses a risk that people, facing many risks, may remain vulnerable and without necessary support (21, 25, 45).[51]

Recent experiences in the world economy led the Pope to call for the renewal of the entire financial system. The purpose of such a system should be to improve wealth creation and promote the genuine development of individuals

48 The Pope is referring in particular to so-called microfinance, including microcredit.

49 The Pope uses here a utilitarian argument, claiming that it is also in the interest of rich countries to achieve this goal (27).

50 The best example of this is the financial crisis that broke out in mid-2007.

51 This applies to both national and international lending.

and nations. This will be possible if not only individual initiatives but the entire system operates based on ethical norms, particularly those proclaimed by the Catholic Church. In this regard, it is worth quoting the words of the Pope, who states: "[A]dhering to the values of Christianity is not merely useful but essential for building a good society and for true integral human development" (4). Concerning the financial system, this means that the goal must be to ensure that the logic of the gift does not contrast with that of economic efficiency and that instruments (including legal ones) need to be created to protect weaker actors, such as savers, from unfavorable or even fraudulent forms of investment and, regarding borrowers, to enable financial support for the most vulnerable while protecting them from usury (65).

3.7. Francis

Pope Francis continues the tradition of Catholic social teaching but places emphasis on prophetic social preaching, particularly in the fields of ecology and the option for the poor.

3.7.1. "Laudato si'"

The question of ecology has been in the spotlight of interest for the Popes since at least Paul VI. However, Pope Francis' encyclical "Laudato si'" is the first document of its kind in the history of the Catholic Church entirely dedicated to the issue of ecology.[52] The aim of the encyclical was to invite a new dialogue on how humanity shapes the future of "our common home," that is, planet Earth (13). The Pope connects the issue of the increasing exploitation of the planet with injustice toward the poor. According to Francis, we cannot avoid recognizing today that a truly ecological approach always becomes a social approach that must integrate justice in environmental discussions, listening to "*both the cry of the earth and the cry of the poor*" (49).[53]

The encyclical contains numerous threads and a variety of methodological approaches that seem to stem from the Pope's conviction that everything in the world is interconnected (16, 70). Although, as in previous encyclicals on the social teaching of the Catholic Church, there is no direct reference to money, Pope

---

52 Pope Francis (2015); Cf. Zenner Peppard (2018, p. 515).

53 However, the Pope sees the main cause of the ecological crisis at a deeper level than politics or economics, namely in the false anthropology of modernity. Cf. Deutsche Bischofskonferenz (2015, p. 4).

Francis refers to it within many threads. With reference to the Pope's call for dialogue, this encyclical can be treated as a voice in such a dialogue, a voice addressing international, national, and economic policies.

Firstly, the question arises of how the Pope perceives the modern world. It seems that the world is divided into two camps: poor countries and rich countries. There is "global inequality" between these two groups (48–52). Poor countries are victims of the policies of rich countries and international economic interests. International politics seems ineffective in combating inequality.[54] Furthermore, the policies of rich countries are not geared toward genuinely helping needy countries, as they are subordinated to an alliance of technology and finances, that is, the direct interests of certain groups. Such policies deal with justifying the present economic system, primarily based on speculation and the pursuit of financial gain, tending to ignore what lies outside economic interests, threatening human dignity, and harming the environment (54–56). In this context, the Pope's conclusion that the current global system is evidently unsustainable under various dimensions seems apparent (61).

Like his predecessors, Francis criticizes international aid programs determined by the introduction of a policy of birth reduction in poor countries, called "reproductive health." However, the Pope goes further and reveals the true cause of the problem. In his view, the global problems of access to and distribution of goods are not the result of excessive population growth in poor countries but of the "extreme and selective consumerism" of the rich. The model of such consumerism cannot be introduced on a global scale, even for this reason alone (and here the Pope returns to his main thought), as it would have devastating consequences for the natural environment, such as enormous waste (50).

The Pope not only focuses on criticizing reality but calls for international solidarity, which should be expressed, among other things, in ensuring that poor countries do not bear the costs of inadequate climate policies of rich countries. He emphasizes that international measures must not burden poor countries with unbearable burdens. For example, the Pope refers to strategies for reducing greenhouse gas emissions that involve internationalizing environmental costs or trading in so-called carbon credits, which, instead of contributing to reducing greenhouse gases, can lead to new forms of speculation.[55] From other

54 The Pope is also aware of positive initiatives on the international level (168). However, it seems that they do not change the negative overall assessment of the present.

55 Carbon credits trading is one of the mechanisms agreed upon under the so-called Kyoto Protocol of 1997. For more information, see, e.g., Yamin (2005).

international activities, the Pope calls for aid to developing countries to be structured so that they have access to technology, technical assistance, and the necessary financial resources to overcome poverty and develop without harming the environment, for example, by using solar energy (169–171).

The interplay between politics and economics has been discussed by many Popes. Pope Francis continues this trend, calling for a description of a policy laden with weaknesses and the demand for a solid, healthy policy. Francis believes that politics is subordinate to the current economic configuration. Above all, large multinational corporations strive to dominate politics (175).

The Pope does not idealize politics; on the contrary, he appears to be critical of it. He observes that politicians are often guided by short-term interests, that is, the maintenance or expansion of power (198). Politicians, especially in poor countries, are susceptible to corruption (142, 197). In democratic countries, they also avoid decisions that are unpopular with voters and interest groups, such as restricting consumption or foreign investments (178).[56] Pope Francis soberly states, "Politics and the economy tend to blame each other when it comes to poverty and environmental degradation. It is to be hoped that they can acknowledge their own mistakes and find forms of interaction directed to the common good" (198).

According to the Pope, it is possible to achieve the goal of real human and societal development not through conflict, competition, and mutual blame but through mutual cooperation and dialogue between politics and the economy. What is the specific role of politics in this cooperation? Francis primarily sees the role as a regulator of the market. The Pope writes, "One authoritative source of oversight and coordination is the law, which lays down rules for admissible conduct in the light of the common good" (177). Secondly, the state should engage in all those areas where the market fails. The Pope mentions many specific areas where the state should intervene. These include promoting forms of industrial production with maximum energy efficiency and reduced resource consumption, removing products that are inefficient in terms of energy consumption or most environmentally polluting from the markets, good traffic management, or construction and modernization techniques that reduce energy consumption and environmental pollution, investments in rural infrastructure, irrigation systems, the development of sustainable agricultural techniques (180).

56 How to heal politics? On the one hand, the Pope appeals to politicians to show themselves as statesmen, and on the other hand, to societies to exert pressure on those in power (178–181).

One of the main problems of the modern world that the Pope addresses is the understanding of the economy and commercial and productive activities, where, according to his criticism, only short-term goals, namely profit maximization at any cost, count (32, 36).

According to the Pope, there is something like a technocratic paradigm that tries to control the sphere of the economy (and indirectly politics). One of the characteristic features of this paradigm is that it treats the surrounding world as a place of conquest. As the Pope metaphorically says, "Human beings and material objects no longer extend a friendly hand to one another; the relationship has become confrontational" (106).

Another determining factor of this approach is the belief in unlimited growth opportunities. It is assumed that this growth will overcome all ecological and social problems. However, the market is not up to this task because this growth in the economic sphere is only associated with the principle of short-term profit maximization. The principle of short-term profit as the only criterion of business activity distorts the concept of the economy. According to this principle, the goal of economic activity is current profit without considering non-economic and future costs. The Pope is particularly concerned that the effects of such activity on humans and the environment, that is, the harm it causes to the social system and the ecosystem, are not taken into account in economic calculations. Thus, economic calculation is distorted because companies only bear a fraction of the costs they themselves cause (36, 109, 195).

Another product of the techno-economic paradigm is compulsive consumerism. This is because the subordinate market tends to create a compulsive consumption mechanism, one that draws people into a whirlpool of unnecessary purchases and expenditures. The Pope writes, "This paradigm leads people to believe that they are free as long as they have the supposed freedom to consume. But those really free are the minority who wield economic and financial power" (203).

According to the Pope, today's market economy is thus a mechanism of human enslavement, turning them into instruments whose goal is to make the few even richer.[57]

The Pope's best understanding of the market seems to be characterized by the words he quotes from one of his previous documents. In such a world, "(…)

57 This gloomy vision of reality ends with the encouraging words of the Pope that not everything is lost, and ecological conversion is possible (205, 216–221).

whatever is fragile, like the environment, is defenceless before the interests of a deified market, which become the only rule" (56).[58]

In addition to the term "deified market," the Pope also uses the term "magical conception of the market." This seems to be an absolutist concept of the market. Accordingly, all problems of the present can be solved by increasing the profits of economic agents or individuals. The Pope neither writes who preaches such a concept nor where exactly such a concept is applied in practice. Such a market concept is harmful because it, among other things, harms humans and the environment. The Pope raises this question with very strong words: "Is it realistic to hope that those who are obsessed with maximizing profits will stop to reflect on the environmental damage which they will leave behind for future generations" (190)?

This question is undoubtedly a form of accusation against proponents of such economic life. The Pope formulates it in a way that gives the impression that, as confirmed by his criticism of the financial system, the entire modern economy lives in a paradigm of profit obsession.

There are also three other economic issues that are constantly present in the social teaching of the Church. These are the issues of work, the universal destination of goods, and the common good.

The question of work repeatedly becomes a topic of papal teaching. The encyclical "Laudato si'" is no exception. The Pope's thought focuses on two themes: financial assistance to the poor in the context of work and the availability of work. The starting point is the universal vocation of humanity to work. Therefore, any financial assistance to the poor should primarily be offered in a way that satisfies only urgent needs but ultimately leads to them being able to live in dignity by earning income from their own work. Financial support should therefore be only a means, not an end in itself. Secondly, the Pope criticizes automation and robotization in the economy. According to the Pope, these phenomena are harmful because they take away jobs from people and thus destroy the so-called social capital and are driven by the "limited interests of business and dubious economic reasoning" (127–128).

Regarding the universal destination of goods, Pope Francis follows in the footsteps of the Church's previous teaching, especially that of John Paul II. The Pope adds that the environment is a common good, that is, it belongs to all of humanity, and all people bear responsibility for it. This does not exclude the possibility that someone could own a portion of it. However, the right to own

58 Quote from: Francis (2013, no. 56).

a portion of the environment does not exempt one from the responsibility to manage it (the Pope speaks of administration) in a way that serves the common good. Those who act only in their own interest burden their consciences by denying the existence of others (93–95).

In the context of the universal destination of goods and their proper use, there is the issue of the common good. The Pope raises the rhetorical question: "What kind of world do we want to leave to those who come after us, to children who are now growing up" (160)? Therefore, the category of the common good is not limited to the dimension of the present generation. The Pope also emphasizes solidarity between generations (159–160). In such a perspective, the question of money and the economy acquires a new, broader dimension. The financial economy cannot be limited to short-term profits, not even within the timeframe of a generation. It should also take into account the benefits and costs of future generations.

Pope Francis seems to have a clearly negative attitude toward banks and the financial system in general. The very strong words he uses in point 189 of his text are significant: "Saving banks at any cost, making the public pay the price, foregoing a firm commitment to reviewing and reforming the entire system, only reaffirms the absolute power of a financial system, a power which has no future and will only give rise to new crises after a slow, costly and only apparent recovery."

The financial crisis of 2007–2008 was an opportunity for the development of a new economy attentive to ethical principles and a regulation of speculative financial activity and fictitious wealth. But there was no reaction that led to a rethinking of the outdated criteria that continue to govern the world" (189).

The Pope assumes that finances exercise almost unlimited power. He claims that they are so powerful that they were saved at any cost. This can be understood to mean that, for example, societies have suffered as a result of rescuing banks. Moreover, there is suspicion that the measures taken to rescue banks and prevent a repeat of the crisis were not effective at all or were only implemented superficially. Secondly, the rules and criteria that guide the functioning of the financial system are outdated and will cause further crises in the future. According to the Pope, the current financial system has no future.

It seems that the Pope takes up financial criticism because he sees a close connection between the financial world and the real economy. And it is not just about finances suffocating the economy; it is also that financial bubbles are often bubbles in the field of production (109, 189). The reason for this is that finances apparently have an influence on the flawed valuation of goods and services in the economy. The Pope writes somewhat mysteriously, "Production is not always rational, and is usually tied to economic variables which assign to products a value that does not necessarily correspond to their real worth" (189).

The Pope's thesis is so general that it is not clear how to understand it. It is only known that the result of such a lack of rationality, according to the Pope, is the "overproduction of certain commodities," which, among other things, leads to environmental damage. Whether production rationality means that supply should be adjusted to demand or demand to supply, and how such adjustment should be regulated, is unknown. It is also not known what the Pope means by "economic variables" that should assign value to products. It is not known whether the Pope understands value in the economic sphere, especially in market exchange, as an objective or subjective value (189).

What alternative and remedy does Francis propose to the criticized economic system? An alternative approach is to the so-called economic ecology, which he generally understands as one that forces us to treat reality more broadly than through the prism of narrowly defined economic calculus (141). In his view, it is necessary to diversify production but also slow down the pace of production and limit consumption so that it corresponds to the requirements of sustainable use of natural resources. And this should not be a compromise between concern for nature and financial revenue or environmental protection and progress. These would be only half-measures that would only delay the catastrophe. The Pope calls for a redefinition of progress so that it leads to a better world and a higher integral quality of life for all people (190–194).

3.7.2. "Fratelli tutti"

In the encyclical "Fratelli tutti," which was signed on October 3, 2020, in Assisi, Pope Francis reflects on brotherhood and social friendship.[59] Although the Pope draws from his Christian beliefs, his primary goal is not to convey Catholic doctrine from the position of the Magisterium but to present thoughts on the universal dimension and openness of social love for all as "a modest contribution to continued reflection" (6). The Pope's desire is for humanity to respond to the challenges of modern times with a dream of brotherhood and social friendship, a dream that goes beyond mere words and leads to actions (6, 8).

As in previous social encyclicals, money is not the central focus of consideration in "Fratelli tutti." Occasional references to money typically appear as quotations from Pope Francis's earlier writings and, therefore, do not introduce new

59 Francis (2020).

concepts beyond what the Pope has previously proclaimed. The only difference lies in the new context in which there are references to money, namely in the context of the universal brotherhood of all humanity.

In "Fratelli tutti," the theme of money primarily emerges in the context of poverty and work. The Pope calls for solidarity among people, addressing the fight against the structural causes of poverty. This includes the fight against inequality, the lack of employment, land, and housing, and the battle against "the destructive effects of the empire of money" (116). It is interesting and important to note the Pope's statement that financial assistance to the poor cannot offer a final solution to their problems but only provides temporary relief. The true solution to the problem of poverty lies in providing opportunities for meaningful work for all (162).

When addressing politicians, the Pope highlights the trend and, at the same time, the danger in the modern world of treating individuals not as humans with dignity and uniqueness but as mere recipients of needs that must be fulfilled. The Pope identifies unmet needs, such as illness, lack of money, or homelessness, as particularly significant. There is a risk that satisfying these needs may become increasingly rationalized, even professionalized, but devoid of brotherly love (193).

Pope Francis criticizes war and renews the call of Pope Paul VI to create a special world fund from the resources allocated for weapons and other military expenditures. This fund would be used to combat hunger and support the development of the poorest countries (262). The Pope strongly condemns terrorism, describing the support of terrorist organizations through the provision of financial resources or the supply of weapons as international crimes that threaten global security and peace (283).

In the first chapter, titled "Dark Clouds over a Closed World," Pope Francis highlights selected tendencies that, as he calls them, hinder the construction of a world of universal brotherhood. One of these phenomena is the way in which economics and finance adopt the expression "opening up to the world" (12). In the Pope's view, this openness is, in practice, a closing off of non-economic values, particularly concerning humanity and human dignity. This kind of openness involves removing barriers and promoting investment freedom for foreign economic powers. It leads to a homogeneous cultural model, a global economy that fails to foster brotherly bonds and instrumentalizes human relationships for the individual interests of the wealthiest and most powerful. The Pope also emphasizes that some wealthy countries or segments of society promote this cultural model among the poor, which can lead to contempt and rejection of what defines the identity and uniqueness of those in poorer countries or social strata. Media and networks, which can be used to pursue the interests of the powerful, play a significant role in this homogenization of the world marked by inequality (52, 166).

This cultural model is particularly exploited by financial speculation and associated exploitation, which, according to Pope Francis, always occurs at the expense of the poor (51–52). In concrete terms, this means that large capital is invested in ways that maximize profits for itself without regard for local interests. Furthermore, the Pope is aware that investments for the weak may not yield as much profit as financial investors expect, hence his call to strengthen government and civil society institutions willing to make such investments. In the context of this cultural model, the Pope's criticism of the technocratic paradigm and particularly individualistic liberal and neoliberal views should be understood.

Pope Francis' main objection to what he calls "forms of liberalism" (155) is that it promotes individualism and serves the economic interests of the rich, making it difficult to think of openness to all, especially to the most vulnerable and to cultural diversity in such a world. Within liberal-individualist views, society is seen only in terms of interests, but without the common ground that Pope calls "roots in a shared narrative" (163). In other words, this form of liberalism is the ideological justification for the tendencies that stand in the way of building a global fraternity.

Therefore, the Pope's alternative is the development of what he calls the "spirit of fraternity." By this, the Pope evidently means an openness and sensitivity to every person in need, expressed through respect for their human dignity, whether they live in the neighborhood or a remote part of the world. It involves the need for effective global organization focused on the common good while also respecting local peculiarities and cultural diversity (165).

Pope Francis appears to criticize neoliberalism and the market in paragraph 168, particularly focusing on criticism of the trickle-down theory.[60] The Pope notes that this approach, which leaves the solution to major social problems in the hands of the market, is not only ineffective in overcoming inequalities and

60 The trickle-down economics (or trickle-down theory) assumes that the market is the best long-term mechanism for redistributing resources. The main idea contained in this theory can be formulated as follows: The state should not prevent individuals from becoming rich, and the wealthiest should bear the relatively lowest fiscal burden because, through their investments and consumer spending, they contribute to the overall economic development of society and increase the prosperity of all people. This is because their purchases create demand in the economy, thereby maintaining and creating jobs. For more details, including an empirical examination, see, e.g., Risch (2023).

unemployment but also hinders the market itself from fully performing its economic functions. Consequently, Pope Francis calls for active economic policies and reforms aimed at freeing politics from the "dictates of finance" (168). This becomes even more significant given the Pope's view that the financial crisis of 2007–2008 not only failed to solve the world's major economic problems but exacerbated them. As the Pope puts it, "Financial speculation fundamentally aimed at quick profit continues to wreak havoc" (168). As a concrete example of the destructive power of the financial world, the Pope cites speculative overvaluation of prices for agricultural products, resulting in not only hunger but even starvation for many people.

Conclusion

What stance does the Catholic Church take on money in its social teachings? The answer to this question is not straightforward. Catholic social teaching has its uniqueness both in terms of its applied methodology and its subject matter. The Church's social teaching is a perspective on reality through the prism of revelation, precisely from the perspective of Scripture and tradition, which also establish the axioms of this teaching. It is therefore based on an unchanging foundation but relates to a constantly changing world. The Church does not claim to possess knowledge in every field. It does not engage in theoretical or practical discussions within specific scientific paradigms or specific systemic solutions. Instead, it attempts to view these matters from the perspective of the human being as a person because the human being is at the center of the Church's social teaching. In this context, the words of John Paul II from "Centesimus annus" are significant: "The Church has no models to present; models that are real and truly effective can only arise within the framework of different historical situations, through the efforts of all those who responsibly confront concrete problems in all their social, economic, political and cultural aspects, as these interact with one another. For such a task the Church offers her social teaching as an indispensable and ideal orientation, a teaching which, as already mentioned, recognizes the positive value of the market and of enterprise, but which at the same time points out that these need to be oriented towards the common good" (43).[1]

In answering the initial question, it must first be established that there is no theory of money in the Church's social teaching. The Church does not make such claims because it goes beyond its competence and mission.

However, this response is only part of the truth. Money accompanies people on their journey in this world. If this is the case, then money must be an object of interest for the Church. More precisely, the Church's consideration of money must pertain to the human being's attitude toward money. The Church shifts the focus from an economic, sociological, political, etc., perspective to an ethical level. Money itself is neither good nor bad; it is neutral, like many other things around us. However, a person's attitude toward money can either allow them and society to develop for the better or lead them astray from the path of development.

1 John Paul II (1991).

In modern Church social teaching, the so-called social encyclicals hold a special place. Although money is not the central subject of consideration in any of these encyclicals, it does not mean that the Popes remain silent on the matter of money.[2] In the first of these social encyclicals, "Rerum novarum," Pope Leo XIII followed the thought of St. Thomas Aquinas and introduced a fundamental principle that concerns all material goods, including money. This principle boils down to the distinction between "just ownership" and the "just use of ownership" (19). Possessing material goods is legitimate, but the principle of the universal destination of goods must not be forgotten. This approach underscores not only the individual but also the social dimension of property. Applied to money, it is permissible to have money, but it is more important to use it correctly. The Christian approach to money is one that is based not only on the principle of justice but also on the principle of charity.

In their encyclicals, the Popes offer a series of considerations regarding specific areas where money can be used for good or ill. These include individual warnings against greed and selfishness, the exclusive focus on material matters, including excessive consumption, and the pursuit of wealth at any cost. On a collective level, there is a warning against absolutizing the economic dimension, that is, making it a goal and a criterion for evaluating the entirety of human life and society. Furthermore, the Popes address issues such as just wages, loans, financial assistance for the poor, including international aid, tax matters, social and property insurance, pricing, interest rates, and the stability of money and the financial system.

Without explicitly delving into aspects like the functions of money or theories of value, the Popes emphasize one crucial point in their social encyclicals: money is just one, albeit very important, means in the economy and society; it essentially forms the circulatory system of the economy. However, it must not become an end to which everything must submit and which everything obeys. When the saying goes, "Money makes the world go round," it clearly expresses the aspect of power associated with money. Power is not inherently bad, but it always requires questioning what is done with that power and who achieves what with the power they possess. In this sense, money must not become a tool of oppression by the wealthy against the poor, and it must not become the primary means of interaction among people. Even as a means, the handling of money requires ethical consideration. The Popes offer important reference points for this through their social principles. Focused on the individual, based on the foundation of

---

2 However, it is surprising that no encyclical refers to Mt 6:24 and the term "Mammon."

solidarity directed toward the common good, and aiming at subsidiarity, money can be an essential element in the humanization of the world.

The Church's teaching on money can be summarized by recalling the thought from the Letter to Titus: "To the clean all things are clean, but to those who are defiled and unbelieving nothing is clean; in fact, both their minds and their consciences are tainted" (Titus 1:15).

References

Alves, A. A., & Moreira, J. M. (2013). *The Salamanca School* (Vol. 9). Bloomsbury Academic.

Anzenbacher, A. (2001). *Einführung in die Ethik*. Patmos-Verl.

Aristotle. (1998). *Politics* (E. Barker, Trans.). Oxford University Press.

Aymans, W. (2015). Betriff, Aufgabe und Träger des Lehramts. In S. Haering, W. Rees, & H. Schmitz (Eds.), *Handbuch des katholischen Kirchenrechts* (Dritte, vollständig neubearbeitete Aufl., pp. 911–921). Verlag Friedrich Pustet.

Aymans, W., Geringer, K.-T., & Schmitz, H. (Eds.). (2017). *Codex des kanonischen Rechtes: Lateinisch-deutsche Ausgabe mit Sachverzeichnis* (8. Aufl.). Verlag Butzon & Bercker.

Azpilcueta, M. (2004). Commentary on the resolution of money. *Journal of Markets & Morality*, *7*(1), 171–312. https://www.marketsandmorality.com/index.php/mandm/article/download/453/443

Baron, A., & Pietras, H. (Eds.). (2003). *Dokumenty soborów powszechnych: Tekst grecki, łaciński, polski: Tom I (325–787)* (Vols. 24, 26, 30, 33). Wydaw. WAM—Księża Jezuici.

Baron, A., & Pietras, H. (Eds.). (2005). *Dokumenty soborów powszechnych: Tekst grecki, łaciński, polski: Tom IV (1511–1870)* (Vols. 24, 26, 30, 33). Wydaw. WAM—Księża Jezuici.

Bauer, D. (2006). *Geldgeschichten der Bibel*. Deutsche Bibelgesellschaft.

Beinert, W. (2017). Lehramt, kirchliches Lehramt. In W. Kasper et al. (Eds.), *Lexikon für Theologie und Kirche* (3. völlig neu bearbeitete Aufl., Sonderausgabe, pp. 751–753). Herder.

Benedict XVI. (2009, June 29). *Caritas in veritate*. The Holy See. https://www.vatican.va/content/benedict-xvi/en/encyclicals/documents/hf_ben-xvi_enc_20090629_caritas-in-veritate.html

Bijleveld, E., & Aarts, H. (Eds.). (2015). *The psychological science of money*. Springer.

Bofinger, P., Reischle, J., & Schächter, A. (2001). *Monetary policy: Goals, institutions, strategies, and instruments*. Oxford University Press.

Bruch, R. (1980). Vitoria. In A. Klose, W. Mantl, & V. Zsifkovits (Eds.), *Katholisches Soziallexikon* (2., gänzl. überarb. und erw. Aufl., pp. 3263–3266). Tyrola.

Brugger, F., & Tackner, N. (2020). Geld als Gegenstand der Sozialwissenschaften. *Soziologische Revue*, *43*(1), 23–38. https://doi.org/10.1515/srsr-2020-0005

Bruin, B., Herzog, L., O'Neill, M., Sandberg, J., & Zalta, E. N. (2018, January 1). *Philosophy of money and finance.* https://plato.stanford.edu/entries/money-finance/

Budzinski, O. (2018, February 19). *Definition: Geld.* https://wirtschaftslexikon.gabler.de/definition/geld-32540

Buechel, E. C., & Morewedge, C. K. (2014). The (relative and absolute) subjective value of money. In E. Bijleveld & H. Aarts (Eds.), *The psychological science of money* (pp. 93–120). Springer. https://doi.org/10.1007/978-1-4939-0959-9_5

Capa, R. L., & Custers, R. (2015). Conscious and unconscious influences of money: Two sides of the same coin? In E. Bijleveld & H. Aarts (Eds.), *The psychological science of money* (pp. 73–91). Springer.

Carter, T. J. (2015). The psychological science of spending money. In E. Bijleveld & H. Aarts (Eds.), *The psychological science of money* (pp. 213–242). Springer.

Catechism of the Catholic Church. (2003, November 4). The Holy See. https://www.vatican.va/archive/ENG0015/_INDEX.HTM

Catholic Church. (1917). *Codex iuris canonici: PII X Pontificis Maximi iussu digestus, Benedicti Papae XV auctoritate promulgatus.* Typis Polyglottis Vaticanis.

Code of Canon Law. (1983, January 25). The Holy See. https://www.vatican.va/archive/cod-iuris-canonici/cic_index_en.html

Congregation for Catholic Education. (1998). *Guidelines for the study and teaching of the Church's Social Doctrine in the formation of Priests.* Office for Publishing and Promotion Services United States Catholic Conference.

Congregation for the Doctrine of the Faith. (1986, March 22). *Instruction on Christian freedom and liberation.* The Holy See. https://www.vatican.va/roman_curia/congregations/cfaith/documents/rc_con_cfaith_doc_19860322_freedom-liberation_en.html

Congregation for the Doctrine of the Faith. (2002, November 24). *Doctrinal note on some questions regarding the participation of Catholics in political life.* The Holy See. https://www.vatican.va/roman_curia/congregations/cfaith/documents/rc_con_cfaith_doc_20021124_politica_en.html

Corkery, P. (2007). *Companion to the compendium of the social doctrine of the Church.* Veritas Publications.

Council Fathers. (1515, May 4). *Fifth Lateran Council 1512–17 A.D.; Session 10: On the reform of credit organisations (Montes pietatis).* Papal Encyclicals. https://www.papalencyclicals.net/councils/ecum18.htm

Council Fathers. (2020, February 20). *First Council of Nicaea—325 AD.* Papal Encyclicals. https://www.papalencyclicals.net/councils/ecum01.htm

Curran, C. E. (2002). *Catholic social teaching, 1891–present: A historical, theological, and ethical analysis*. Georgetown University Press.

Curran, C. E., Himes, K. R., & Shannon, T. A. (2005). Sollicitudo rei socialis. In K. R. Himes (Ed.), *Modern Catholic social teaching: Commentaries and interpretations* (pp. 415–435). Georgetown University Press.

Davies, G. (2002). *A history of money: From ancient times to the present day* (3rd ed., with revisions). University of Wales Press. https://permalink.obvsg.at/AC00953716

Deck, A. F. (2005). Populorum progressio. In K. R. Himes (Ed.), *Modern Catholic social teaching: Commentaries and interpretations* (pp. 292–314). Georgetown University Press.

Deflem, M. (2003). The sociology of the sociology of money: Simmel and the contemporary battle of the classics. *Journal of Classical Sociology*, *3*(1), 67–96. https://doi.org/10.1177/1468795X03003001695

Dembinski, P. H. (2017). *Ethik und Verantwortung im Finanzsektor: Was jetzt zu tun ist*. Schäffer-Poeschel. https://doi.org/10.34156/9783791038650

Deutsche Bischofskonferenz. (2015, June 18). *18.06.2015: Inhaltsangabe der Enzyklika von Papst Franziskus: "Laudato si'—Über die Sorge für das gemeinsame Haus."* https://www.dbk.de/fileadmin/redaktion/diverse_downloads/presse_2015/2015-Enzyklika-Laudato-si-Inhaltsangabe.pdf

Distelhorst, L., Isberner, K., & Schneider, M.-S. (Eds.). (2014). *Leistung: Das Endstadium der Ideologie: Bd. 18*. transcript.

Dodd, N. (2016). *The social life of money*. Princeton University Press. https://doi.org/10.1515/9781400880867

Döpfner, J. (1967). *Schreiben der deutschen Bischöfe an alle, die von der Kirche mit der Glaubensverkündigung beauftragt sind*. https://www.dbk.de/fileadmin/redaktion/veroeffentlichungen/deutsche-bischoefe/DB_0-1.pdf

Drabińska, D. (2020). Fetyszyzm towarowy. In *Encyklopedia PWN*. https://encyklopedia.pwn.pl/haslo/fetyszyzm-towarowy;3900620.html

Drumm, J. (2017). Communio: I. Systematisch-theologisch. In W. Kasper et al. (Eds.), *Lexikon für Theologie und Kirche* (3. völlig neu bearbeitete Aufl., Sonderausgabe, pp. 1280–1283). Herder.

Düwell, M., Hübenthal, C., & Werner, M. H. (2011). *Handbuch Ethik*. J. B. Metzler'sche Verlagsbuchhandlung und Carl Ernst Poeschel Verlag GmbH.

Espeland, W. N., & Stevens, M. L. (1998). Commensuration as a social process. *Annual Review of Sociology*, *24*, 313–343. www.jstor.org/stable/223484

European Central Bank (Ed.). (2011). *The monetary policy of the ECB, 2011* (3rd ed.). European Central Bank. https://www.ecb.europa.eu/pub/pdf/other/monetarypolicy2011en.pdf

Figge, F., & Schaltegger, S. (2000). *Was ist "Stakeholder Value"? Vom Schlagwort zur Messung*. Universität Lüneburg. http://www2.leuphana.de/umanagement/csm/content/nama/downloads/download_publikationen/02-3downloadversion.pdf

Finn, D. (2005). Centesimus annus. In K. R. Himes (Ed.), *Modern Catholic social teaching: Commentaries and interpretations* (pp. 436–466). Georgetown University Press.

Firer Hinze, C. (2005). Quadragesimo anno. In K. R. Himes (Ed.), *Modern Catholic social teaching: Commentaries and interpretations* (pp. 151–174). Georgetown University Press.

Fiske, A. P. (1992). The four elementary forms of sociality: Framework for a unified theory of social relations. *Psychological Review*, *99*(4), 689–723. https://doi.org/10.1037/0033-295X.99.4.689

Francis. (2013, November 24). *Evangelii Gaudium [Apostolic exhortation]*. The Holy See. https://www.vatican.va/content/francesco/en/apost_exhortations/documents/papa-francesco_esortazione-ap_20131124_evangelii-gaudium.html

Francis. (2015, May 24). *Laudato si'*. The Holy See. https://www.vatican.va/content/francesco/en/encyclicals/documents/papa-francesco_20150524_enciclica-laudato-si.html

Francis. (2020, March 10). *Fratelli tutti*. The Holy See. https://www.vatican.va/content/francesco/en/encyclicals/documents/papa-francesco_20201003_enciclica-fratelli-tutti.html

Frisby, D. (1984). Georg Simmels Theorie der Moderne. In H.-J. Dahme & O. Rammstedt (Eds.), *Georg Simmel und die Moderne: Neue Interpretationen und Materialien* (1. Aufl., Vol. 469, pp. 9–79). Suhrkamp.

Furnham, A. (2014). *The new psychology of money* (1. publ). Routledge.

Gaillardetz, R. R. (2005). The ecclesiological foundations of modern Catholic social teaching. In K. R. Himes (Ed.), *Modern Catholic social teaching: Commentaries and interpretations* (pp. 75–98). Georgetown University Press.

Gerdesmeier, D. (2006). *Geldtheorie und Geldpolitik: Eine praxisorientierte Einführung* (2nd ed.). Bankakad.-Verl.

Gischer, H., Herz, B., & Menkhoff, L. (2020). *Geld, Kredit und Banken: Eine Einführung* (4th ed.). Springer Gabler. https://doi.org/10.1007/978-3-662-49227-7

Goodchild, P. (2009). *Theology of money*. Duke University Press.

Goodchild, P. (2010). The market, god, and the ascetic life. In I. Pyysiäinen (Ed.), *Religion, economy, and cooperation* (Vol. 49, pp. 219–236). De Gruyter. https://doi.org/10.1515/9783110246339.219

Heinsohn, G., & Steiger, O. (2006). The property theory of interest and money. In J. N. Smithin (Ed.), *What is money?* (Transferred to digital printing 2006, Vol. 6, pp. 67–100). Routledge.

Hellmich, W. (2013). *Aufklärende Rationalisierung: Ein Versuch, Max Weber neu zu interpretieren* (1st ed., Vol. 107). Duncker & Humblot. https://doi.org/10.3790/978-3-428-53906-2

Hicks, J. (1967). *Critical essays in monetary theory*. Clarendon Press. https://permalink.obvsg.at/UGR/AC00195792

Himes, K. R. (2005a). Introduction. In K. R. Himes (Ed.), *Modern Catholic social teaching: Commentaries and interpretations* (pp. 1–6). Georgetown University Press.

Himes, K. R. (Ed.). (2005b). *Modern Catholic social teaching: Commentaries and interpretations*. Georgetown University Press.

Höffe, O. (2006). *Mała historia filozofii*. Wydawnictwo Naukowe PWN.

Huberfeld, R., & Dannon, P. N. (2015). Pathological gambling: Who gains from others' losses? In E. Bijleveld & H. Aarts (Eds.), *The psychological science of money* (pp. 163–185). Springer.

Ingham, G. K. (2004). *The nature of money* (1. publ). Polity Press.

Ingham, G. K. (2006). "Babylonian madness": On the historical and sociological origins of money. In J. N. Smithin (Ed.), *What is money?* (Transferred to digital printing 2006, Vol. 6, pp. 16–41). Routledge.

International Monetary Fund. (2023a). *Annual report on exchange arrangements and exchange restrictions 2022*. https://www.elibrary.imf.org/display/book/9798400235269/9798400235269.xml

International Monetary Fund. (2023b). *Special drawing rights*. https://www.imf.org/en/Topics/special-drawing-right

Issing, O. (1993). Geld. In G. Enderle, K. Homan, M. Honecker, W. Kerber, & H. Steinmann (Eds.), *Lexikon der Wirtschaftsethik* (pp. 331–335). Herder.

Issing, O. (2007). *Einführung in die Geldtheorie* (14., wesentl. überarb. Aufl.). Vahlen.

Jarchow, H.-J. (2010). *Grundriss der Geldtheorie: Vol. 3339: Wirtschaftswissenschaften* (12., neu bearb. und erw. Aufl.). Lucius & Lucius.

John Paul II. (1984). *Reconciliatio et Paenitentia [Post-synodal Apostolic exhortation]*. The Holy See. https://www.vatican.va/content/john-paul-ii/en/apost_

exhortations/documents/hf_jp-ii_exh_02121984_reconciliatio-et-paeniten tia.html

John Paul II. (1981, September 14). *Laborem exercens*. The Holy See. https://www.vatican.va/content/john-paul-ii/en/encyclicals/documents/hf_jp-ii_enc_14091981_laborem-exercens.html

John Paul II. (1987, December 30). *Sollicitudo Rei Socialis*. The Holy See. https://www.vatican.va/content/john-paul-ii/en/encyclicals/documents/hf_jp-ii_enc_30121987_sollicitudo-rei-socialis.html

John Paul II. (1991, January 5). *Centesimus Annus*. The Holy See. https://www.vatican.va/content/john-paul-ii/en/encyclicals/documents/hf_jp-ii_enc_01051991_centesimus-annus.html

John Paul II. (1995, March 25). *Evangelium Vitae*. The Holy See. https://www.vatican.va/content/john-paul-ii/en/encyclicals/documents/hf_jp-ii_enc_25031995_evangelium-vitae.html

John Paul II. (2004a, January 1). *Message of his holiness Pope John Paul II for the celebration of the world day of peace*. The Holy See. https://www.vatican.va/content/john-paul-ii/en/messages/peace/documents/hf_jp-ii_mes_20031216_xxxvii-world-day-for-peace.html

John Paul II. (2004b, February 4). *General audience: Wednesday, 4 February 2004*. The Holy See. https://www.vatican.va/content/john-paul-ii/en/audiences/2004/documents/hf_jp-ii_aud_20040204.html

John XXIII. (1961, May 15). *Mater et Magistra*. The Holy See. https://www.vatican.va/content/john-xxiii/en/encyclicals/documents/hf_j-xxiii_enc_15051961_mater.html

John XXIII. (1963, November 4). *Pacem in Terris*. The Holy See. https://www.vatican.va/content/john-xxiii/en/encyclicals/documents/hf_j-xxiii_enc_11041963_pacem.html

Johnson, L. (2011). *Everything the Bible says about money*. Bethany House Publishers.

Kaiser, W. C., Bruce, F. F., Davids, P. H., & Brauch, M. T. (1996). *Hard sayings of the Bible*. IVP Academic.

Kant, I. (1902). *Kritik der reinen Vernunft (1. Aufl. 1781); Prolegomena; Grundlegung zur Metaphysik der Sitten; Metaphysische Anfangsgründe der Naturwissenschaften* (Vol. 4). De Gruyter.

Kant, I. (1998). *Groundwork of the metaphysics of morals* (M. J. Gregor, Trans.). Cambridge University Press.

Katholischer Erwachsenen-Katechismus: Das Glaubensbekenntnis der Kirche (5. Aufl., Vol. 1). (1985). Herder.

Katholischer Erwachsenen-Katechismus: Leben aus dem Glauben (Vol. 2). (1995). Herder.

Klose, A. (1979). *Die katholische Soziallehre: Ihr Anspruch, ihre Aktualität*. Verlag Styria.

Knapp, G. F. (1918). *Staatliche Theorie des Geldes* (2. Aufl., durchges. und verm). Duncker & Humblot. https://nbn-resolving.org/urn:nbn:de:s2w-6471

Knoblauch, H. (2006). *Sozialtechnologie, Soziologie und Rhetorik: Manuskript*. http://www.as.tu-berlin.de/fileadmin/fg225/material_knoblauch/knoblauch_2006_Sozialtechnologie.pdf

Kramer, R. (1996). *Ethik des Geldes: Eine theologische und ökonomische Verhältnisbestimmung* (Vol. 31). Duncker & Humblot.

Krucina, J. (2010). O dobro wspólne zglobalizowanego świata. In Benedykt XVI, *Caritas in Veritate* (pp. 153–197). TUM.

Krug, M. K., & Braver, T. S. (2015). Motivation and Cognitive Control: Going Beyond Monetary Incentives. In E. Bijleveld & H. Aarts (Eds.), *The psychological science of money* (pp. 137–162). Springer.

Lamoureux, P. A. (2005). Laborem exercens. In K. R. Himes (Ed.), *Modern Catholic social teaching: Commentaries and interpretations* (pp. 389–414). Georgetown University Press.

Lapatsioras, S., & Milios, J. (2012). The notion of money from the "Grundrisse" to "capital." *Science & Society*, *76*(4), 521–545. www.jstor.org/stable/41714355

Lau, M., Bauks, M., Koenen, K., & Alkier Stefan. (2013, January 1). *Numismatik*. https://www.bibelwissenschaft.de/fileadmin/buh_bibelmodul/media/wibi/pdf/Numismatik__2018-09-20_06_20.pdf

Lea, S. E. G., & Webley, P. (2006). Money as tool, money as drug: The biological psychology of a strong incentive. *The Behavioral and Brain Sciences*, *29*(2), 161–209. https://doi.org/10.1017/S0140525X06009046

Lea, S. E. G., & Webley, P. (2015). Money: Metaphors and motives. In E. Bijleveld & H. Aarts (Eds.), *The psychological science of money* (pp. 21–35). Springer.

Leo X. (1901_1927). Inter multiplices: Concilium Lateranense V. In G. D. Mansi (Ed.), *Sacrorum conciliorum nova et amplissima collectio* (Vol. 32, pp. 905–907). H. Welter.

Leo XIII. (2007). Enzyklika Rerum novarum (15.05.1891). In KAB, Katholische Arbeitnehmer-Bewegung Deutschlands e.V. (Ed.), *Texte zur katholischen Soziallehre: Die sozialen Rundschreiben der Päpste und andere kirchliche Dokumente* (9., erw. Aufl., pp. 1–40). Butzon & Bercker; Ketteler.

Leo XIII. (1891a, May 15). *Litterae Encyclicae Rerum Novarum*. The Holy See. http://www.vatican.va/content/leo-xiii/la/encyclicals/documents/hf_l-xiii_enc_15051891_rerum-novarum.html

Leo XIII. (1891b, May 15). *Rerum Novarum*. The Holy See. http://www.vatican.va/content/leo-xiii/en/encyclicals/documents/hf_l-xiii_enc_15051891_rerum-novarum.html

Leo XIII. (1899, September 18). *Paternae*. The Holy See. http://w2.vatican.va/content/leo-xiii/en/encyclicals/documents/hf_l-xiii_enc_18091899_paternae.html

Leo XIII. (1902, October 22). *Quae ad Nos*. The Holy See. http://w2.vatican.va/content/leo-xiii/en/encyclicals/documents/hf_l-xiii_enc_22111902_quae-ad-nos.html

Lütge, C., & Uhl, M. (2017). *Wirtschaftsethik*. Verlag Franz Vahlen GmbH. https://doi.org/10.15358/9783800652457

Majka, J. (1986). *Katolicka nauka społeczna: Studium historyczno-doktrynalne*. Fundacja Jana Pawła II. Polski Instytut Kultury Chrześcijańskiej.

Majka, J. (1996). Nauka społeczna Kościoła, jej charakter i miejsce w orędziu ewangelicznym. In M. Radwan et al. (Eds.), *Dokumenty nauki społecznej Kościoła* (2nd ed., pp. 11–58). Redakcja Wydawnictw Katolickiego Uniwersytetu Lubelskiego.

Marx, K. (1989). ERSTER ABSCHNITT. Waare und Geld. In W. Bang, R. Hecker, Edgar, E. Kopf, et al. (Eds.), *Karl Marx: Das Kapital. Kritik der politischen Ökonomie. Erster Band, Hamburg 1883 // Gesamtausgabe (MEGA)* (pp. 63–162). De Gruyter Akademie Forschung. https://doi.org/10.1515/9783050076553-008

May, G. (2017). Enzyklika. In W. Kasper et al. (Eds.), *Lexikon für Theologie und Kirche* (3. völlig neu bearbeitete Aufl., Sonderausgabe, pp. 697–698). Herder.

Mead, N. L., & Stuppy, A. (2015). Two sides of the same coin: money can promote and hinder interpersonal processes. In E. Bijleveld & H. Aarts (Eds.), *The psychological science of money*. Springer.

Menger, C. (1936). *The collected works of Carl Menger, vol. IV: Schriften Über Geldtheorie und Währungspolitik*. Percy Lund, Humphries & Co. https://www.mises.at/static/literatur/Buch/menger-schriften-ueber-geldtheorie-und-waehrungspolitik.pdf

Menger, C., & Braumüller, W. (1871). *Grundsätze der Volkswirtschaftslehre*. Online Library of Liberty. https://oll.libertyfund.org/titles/1279

Mich, M. L. (2005a). Mater et magistra. In K. R. Himes (Ed.), *Modern Catholic social teaching: Commentaries and interpretations* (pp. 191–216). Georgetown University Press.

Mich, M. L. (2005b). Mater et magistra. In K. R. Himes (Ed.), *Modern Catholic social teaching: Commentaries and interpretations* (pp. 191–216). Georgetown University Press.

Minch, D. (2018). What kind of god is money anyway? An Investigation into the theological structures of capitalism and Gnosticism. *Interdisciplinary Journal for Religion and Transformation in Contemporary Society (J-RaT)*, *4*(2), 62–83. https://doi.org/10.14220/jrat.2018.4.2.62

Molina, L. (2015). *A treatise on money*. Christian's Library Press.

Moller, A. C., & Deci, E. L. (2015). The psychology of getting paid: An integrated perspective. In E. Bijleveld & H. Aarts (Eds.), *The psychological science of money*. Springer.

Nell-Breuning, O. (1962). *Vom Geld und vom Kapital* (Vol. 134). Herder.

Nell-Breuning, O. (1977). *Soziallehre der Kirche: Erläuterungen der lehramtlichen Dokumente* (Vol. 5). Europaverl.

Neuhold, L. (2000). *Religion und katholische Soziallehre im Wandel vor allem der Werte: Erscheinungsbilder und Chancen* (Vol. 43). Lit.

Nitecki, P. (2010). Posłowie. In Benedykt XVI, *Caritas in Veritate* (pp. 199–214). TUM.

Parsons, T. (1951). *The social system: The major exposition of the author's conceptual scheme for the analysis of the dynamics, of the social system*. The Free Press.

Paul, A. T. (2012). *Die Gesellschaft des Geldes: Entwurf einer monetären Theorie der Moderne* (2., erweiterte Aufl.). VS Verlag für Sozialwissenschaften. https://doi.org/10.1007/978-3-531-18900-0

Paul VI. (1964, April 12). *Journey to India. Address to the press*. The Holy See. https://www.vatican.va/content/paul-vi/en/speeches/1964/documents/hf_p-vi_spe_19641204_press.html

Paul VI. (1967, March 26). *Populorum Progressio*. The Holy See. https://www.vatican.va/content/paul-vi/en/encyclicals/documents/hf_p-vi_enc_26031967_populorum.html

Paul VI. (1968, January 1). *I world day for peace 1968: The day of peace*. The Holy See. https://www.vatican.va/content/paul-vi/en/messages/peace/documents/hf_p-vi_mes_19671208_i-world-day-for-peace.html

Paul VI. (1969, January 1). *II world day for peace 1969: The promotion of human rights, the way to Peace*. The Holy See. https://www.vatican.va/content/paul-vi/en/messages/peace/documents/hf_p-vi_mes_19681208_ii-world-day-for-peace.html

Pfreundschuh, W. (2020, March 16). *Warenfetischismus*. https://kulturkritik.net/begriffe/begr_txt.php?lex=warenfetisch

Pius XI. (1931a, May 15). *Litterae Encyclicae Quadragesimo anno*. The Holy See. http://www.vatican.va/content/pius-xi/la/encyclicals/documents/hf_p-xi_enc_19310515_quadragesimo-anno.html

Pius XI. (1931b, May 15). *Quadragesimo Anno*. The Holy See. https://www.vatican.va/content/pius-xi/en/encyclicals/documents/hf_p-xi_enc_19310515_quadragesimo-anno.html

Pius XI. (1932, March 5). *Caritate Christi Compulsi*. The Holy See. https://www.vatican.va/content/pius-xi/en/encyclicals/documents/hf_p-xi_enc_03051932_caritate-christi-compulsi.html

Pius XI. (1937, March 19). *Divini Redemptoris*. The Holy See. https://www.vatican.va/content/pius-xi/en/encyclicals/documents/hf_p-xi_enc_19370319_divini-redemptoris.html

Pius XII. (1944, December 24). *Radio message "Benignitas et humanitas" for Christmas*. The Holy See. https://www.vatican.va/content/pius-xii/en/speeches/1944/documents/hf_p-xii_spe_19441224_natale.html

Piwowarczyk, J. (1946). Wstęp. In Pius XI, *Quadragesimo anno* (2nd ed., pp. 1–9). Verbum.

Plato. (1998). *Republic*. Oxford University Press.

Polanyi, K. (1978). *The great transformation: Politische und ökonomische Ursprünge von Gesellschaften und Wirtschaftssystemen* (1. Aufl., Vol. 260). Suhrkamp.

Pontifical Council for Justice and Peace. (2006). *Compendium of the social doctrine of the Church*. The Holy See. https://www.vatican.va/roman_curia/pontifical_councils/justpeace/documents/rc_pc_justpeace_doc_20060526_compendio-dott-soc_en.html

Reifner, U. (2017). *Das Geld: Band 2 Soziologie des Geldes—Heuristik und Mythos*. Springer Fachmedien Wiesbaden; Imprint Springer VS. https://doi.org/10.1007/978-3-658-14104-2

Retzbach, A. (1953). *Das Recht der katholischen Kirche nach dem Codex Iuris Canonici: Für die Praxis bearbeitet* (F. Vetter, Ed.; 4th ed.). Herder. https://permalink.obvsg.at/UGR/AC05242777

Rich, A. (1992). *Wirtschaftsethik: Band II: Marktwirtschaft, Planwirtschaft, Weltwirtschaft aus sozialethischer Sicht* (2nd ed.). Gütersloher Verl.-Haus Mohn.

Riedel-Spangenberger, I. (2017). Lehramt, kirchliches Lehramt: IV. Kirchenrechtlich. In W. Kasper et al. (Eds.), *Lexikon für Theologie und Kirche* (3. völlig neu bearbeitete Aufl., Sonderausgabe, pp. 753–754). Herder.

Risch, M. (2023). Trickle-down revisited. *Oxford Review of Economic Policy, 39*(3), 498–512. https://doi.org/10.1093/oxrep/grad023

Rodziński, A. (1960). *Sprawiedliwość chrześcijańska wobec problemu nierówności majątkowych w II i III wieku* (Vol. 14). Towarzystwo Naukowe Katolickiego Uniwersytetu Lubelskiego.

Roos, L. (2008). Die Sozialenzykliken der Päpste. In A. Rauscher (Ed.), *Handbuch der Katholischen Soziallehre* (pp. 125–142). Duncker & Humblot.

Saint Augustine. (2008a). *The city of god, Books I–VII* (Issue v. 8). Catholic University of America Press; eBook Academic Collection (EBSCOhost). https://search.ebscohost.com/login.aspx?direct=true&db=e000xww&AN=498860&lang=pl&site=ehost-live

Saint Augustine. (2008b). *The city of god, Books VIII–XVI* (Issue v. 14). Catholic University of America Press; eBook Academic Collection (EBSCOhost). https://search.ebscohost.com/login.aspx?direct=true&db=e000xww&AN=498863&lang=pl&site=ehost-live

Saint Leo the Great. (1957). Letter 4: To the bishops residing in Campania, Piceno, Etruria, and all provinces. In *Letters* (Issue v. 34, pp. 23–27). Catholic University of America Press; eBook Academic Collection (EBSCOhost). https://search.ebscohost.com/login.aspx?direct=true&db=e000xww&AN=498899&lang=pl&site=ehost-live

Samanez-Larkin, G. R., Hagen, T. A., & Weiner, D. J. (2015). Financial decision making across adulthood. In E. Bijleveld & H. Aarts (Eds.), *The psychological science of money* (pp. 121–135). Springer.

Schmitz, W. (2004). *Wirtschaftsethik als Ordnungsethik: In ihrem Anspruch an Sozial-, Konjunktur- und Währungspolitik* (J. H. Pichler & S. W. Schmitz, Eds.; 1st ed., Vol. 537). Duncker & Humblot. https://doi.org/10.3790/978-3-428-51341-3

Schuck, M. J. (1991). *That they be one: The social teaching of the papal encyclicals, 1740–1989*. Georgetown University Press.

Schwindt, D. (2015). *Catholic social teaching: A new synthesis: Rerum Novarum to Laudato Si'*. Agnus Dei Publishing.

Shannon, T. A. (2005). Rerum novarum. In K. R. Himes (Ed.), *Modern Catholic social teaching: Commentaries and interpretations* (pp. 127–150). Georgetown University Press.

Simmel, G. (2005). *The philosophy of money* (3rd enlarged ed.). Routledge.

Simmel, G. (2009). *Philosophie des Geldes* (Nachdr. [der Ausg.] Leipzig, Duncker&Humblot, 1907, 2., verm. Aufl.). Anaconda.

Smith, A. (1776). *An inquiry into the nature and causes of the wealth of nations.* Printed for W. Strahan; and T. Cadell in the Strand; JSTOR. https://jstor.org/stable/community.34338280

Smithin, J. N. (Ed.). (2006). *What is money?* (Transferred to digital printing 2006, Vol. 6). Routledge.

Stryczek, J. (2015). *Pieniądze: W świetle Ewangelii. Nowa opowieść o biedzie i zarabianiu*. Wydawnictwo Literackie.

Strzeszewski, C. (2003). *Katolicka nauka społeczna* (4th ed.). Wydaw. KUL.

Szewczyk, R. (2020). *Podstawy ekonomii personalistycznej*. http://www.szewczyk.net.pl/wp-content/uploads/2020/03/Podstawy-ekonomii-personalistycznej.pdf

Taylor, C. (2007). *A secular age* (First Harvard University Press paperback edition). The Belknap Press of Harvard University Press.

Taylor, J. B., & Weerapana, A. (2010). *Economics* (6th internat. ed., financial crisis updated ed.). South-Western, Cengage Learning.

The Holy See. (1983, October 22). *Charter of the rights of the family*. The Holy See. https://www.vatican.va/roman_curia/pontifical_councils/family/documents/rc_pc_family_doc_19831022_family-rights_en.html

Thomas Aquinas. (1981). *Summa theologica* (Fathers of the English Dominican Province, Trans.; Complete English ed.). Christian Classics. https://aquinas101.thomisticinstitute.org/st-index

Vatican Council II. (1964, November 21). *Lumen gentium*. The Holy See. https://www.vatican.va/archive/hist_councils/ii_vatican_council/documents/vat-ii_const_19641121_lumen-gentium_en.html

Vatican Council II. (1965a, July 12). *Dignitatis humanae*. The Holy See. https://www.vatican.va/archive/hist_councils/ii_vatican_council/documents/vat-ii_decl_19651207_dignitatis-humanae_en.html

Vatican Council II. (1965b, July 12). *Gaudium et spes*. The Holy See. https://www.vatican.va/archive/hist_councils/ii_vatican_council/documents/vat-ii_const_19651207_gaudium-et-spes_en.html

Vatican Radio. (2010, June 28). *Pope announces new pontifical council to re-Evangelise secularized Christian nations*. Vatican Radio. https://www.archivioradiovaticana.va/storico/2010/06/28/pope_announces_new_pontifical_council_to_re-evangelise_secularized/en1-404174

Vermeersch, A. (1912). Usury. In *The Catholic encyclopedia*. Robert Appleton Company. https://www.newadvent.org/cathen/15235c.htm

Vohs, K. D., Mead, N. L., & Goode, M. R. (2006). The psychological consequences of money. *Science, 314*(5802), 1154–1156. https://doi.org/10.1126/science.1132491

Vohs, K. D., Mead, N. L., & Goode, M. R. (2008). Merely activating the concept of money changes personal and interpersonal behavior. *Current*

Directions in Psychological Science, *17*(3), 208–212. https://doi.org/10.1111/j.1467-8721.2008.00576.x

Walsh, A. J., & Lynch, T. (2008). *The morality of money: An exploration in analytic philosophy / Adrian Walsh and Tony Lynch*. Palgrave Macmillan.

Walsh, C. E. (2003). *Monetary theory and policy* (2nd ed.). MIT Press.

Wariboko, N. (2008). *God and money: A theology of money in a globalizing world*. Lexington Books.

Weber, M. (1978). *Economy and society: An outline of interpretive sociology* (G. Roth & C. Wittich, Eds.). University of California Press.

Weber, M. (2013). *Protestant ethic and the spirit of capitalism*. Taylor and Francis.

Weiler, R. (1991). *Einführung in die katholische Soziallehre: Ein systematischer Abriß*. Verlag Styria.

Woeckener, B. (2020). *Mikroökonomik: Eine Einführung* (4th ed.). Springer Berlin Heidelberg; Imprint Springer Gabler. https://doi.org/10.1007/978-3-662-60668-1

Woll, A. (Ed.). (2008). *Wirtschaftslexikon: Jubiläumsausgabe* (10., vollst. neubearb. Aufl.). Oldenbourg Wissenschaftsverlag. https://doi.org/10.1524/9783486847581

Wray, L. R. (1998). *Money and taxes: The Chartalist approach* (Working Paper, 222). http://www.levyinstitute.org/pubs/wp222.pdf

Yamin, F. (Ed.). (2005). *Climate change and carbon markets: A handbook of emission reduction mechanisms*. Earthscan.

Zenner Peppard, C. (2018). Commentary on Laudato si' (On care for our common home). In K. R. Himes, L. S. Cahill, C. E. Curran, D. Hollenbach, & T. A. Shannon (Eds.), *Modern Catholic social teaching: Commentaries and interpretations* (2nd ed., pp. 515–550). Georgetown University Press.

Zsifkovits, V. (1990). Grundprinzipien der katholischen Soziallehre. *Theologisch-Praktische Quartalschrift*, *138*, 16–25.

Polish Studies in Economics

Edited by Ryszard Kokoszczyński

Vol. 1	Wojciech Grabowski: Employee Stock Options, Payout Policy, and Stock Returns. Shareholders and Option Holders in Large U.S. Technology Corporations. 2012.
Vol. 2	Jan Jakub Michałek/Michał Brzozowski/Andrzej Cieślik (eds.): The Relationship between Human Development, Exports and Foreign Direct Investments in Emerging Europe. 2013.
Vol. 3	Tomasz Żylicz: The Economics of International Environmental Cooperation. 2015.
Vol. 4	Juliusz Jabłecki / Ryszard Kokoszczyński / Paweł Sakowski / Robert Ślepaczuk / Piotr Wójcik: Volatility as an Asset Class. Obvious Benefits and Hidden Risks. 2015.
Vol. 5	Janusz Kudła / Konrad Walczyk / Robert Kruszewski / Katarzyna Kopczewska / Agata Kocia: Modeling Fiscal Policy in the European Union. 2015.
Vol. 6	Andrzej Cieślik / Jan Jakub Michałek (eds.): Liberalization of Transportation Services in the EU: the Polish Perspective. 2015.
Vol. 7	Katarzyna Metelska-Szaniawska: Economic Effects of Post-Socialist Constitutions 25 Years from the Outset of Transition. The Constitutional Political Economy Approach. 2016.
Vol. 8	Elżbieta Czarny / Andżelika Kuźnar / Jerzy Menkes (eds.): The Impact of the Transatlantic Trade and Investment Partnership on International Cooperation. 2017.
Vol. 9	Adam Czarnecki: Going Local? Linking and Integrating Second-Home Owners with the Community's Economy. A Comparative Study between Finnish and Polish Second-Home Owners. 2017.
Vol. 10	Adam Biela (ed.): European Questionnaire for Job Analysis (EQJA). 2018.
Vol. 11	Gabriela Grotkowska: Public-Sector Wage Premium in Poland. 2018.
Vol. 12	Piotr Dybka: What Determines International Competitiveness of the Economy? Evidence from Bayesian Model Averaging. 2022.
Vol. 13	Damian Bębnowski: The Importance of Constitutional Rules and Property Rights. The German Economy in 1990–2015. 2022.
Vol. 14	Wojciech Łątkowski: Projections of Demand for Care among the Elderly in Poland Including Health Status and Living Arrangements. 2024.
Vol. 15	Dominik J. Gajewski (ed.): *VAT Gap* in Poland: Policy Problem and Policy Response. 2024.
Vol. 16	Piotr Karaś: Money in Modern Social Encyclicals. 2024.

www.peterlang.com

www.ingramcontent.com/pod-product-compliance
Ingram Content Group UK Ltd.
Pitfield, Milton Keynes, MK11 3LW, UK
UKHW021833100926
8556IPUK00004B/314